DON'T SHOW YOUR UNDERWARE!

# DON'T SHOW YOUR UNDERWARE!

## *Making Your Presentations Work*

### TOM LAURENSON

CONNECTICUT 2023

Book Design by Jennifer Payne (Words by Jen, Branford, CT)

Paperback   ISBN 978-1-7370046-1-5
ePub          ISBN 978-1-7370046-2-2

For more information, please visit www.tomlaurenson.com.

# DEDICATION

This book has evolved over a number of years, and incorporates a wealth of presentation experience and observation. I am happy to dedicate this book to…

My wife, Alice Laurenson, for her patient proofreading and steadfast encouragement.

My good friend and colleague, Ian Gowdie, for his superb illustrations.

The late Sue Morrow Flanagan for her constant support despite her battle with cancer.

Those friends and colleagues who read early drafts and offered criticism and advice.

The many presenters and audiences whose efforts
and experiences have been inspirational.

Despite best efforts, there may remain errors, for which the blame is entirely mine.

*Tom Laurenson*
Branford, Connecticut

# CONTENTS

# Preface

Presentations are important. Did you get that job or promotion? Did you make that sale? Did you win over public opinion? Did you persuade your organization to do something? So often, people don't succeed in these areas because of a lack of presentation skills.

I wrote this book after seeing so many presentations that didn't fulfill their purpose due to basic errors or omissions. I looked at a range of books on presentations. Most defined an approach or style and didn't get down to the basics that so many people needed. Over the years I learned from every presentation I undertook, from every error I made, and collected observations.

This book is the result and offers a range of suggestions and options from which you can choose to suit your individual personality, match your personal style, and fit your situation, and it offers help in areas that most books on presentation avoid or omit.

That's what makes this book an invaluable companion for the modern presenter. Enjoy the journey.

Tom Laurenson
Branford, Connecticut

Author of *59 Ideas for the Digital Camera in the Classroom* and *Sound Ideas for the Classroom*

x

# Introduction

You struggled with that last college presentation, and they didn't take you. You did your best at that job interview, but didn't get it. You tried to sell that idea to your colleagues (or your employees), but they still don't understand. You are arguing with management over working conditions, but they don't see what the problem is. You know you deserve a raise, or a promotion, but don't know how to ask for it. You can't persuade the School Board to do the right thing. You are trying to get elected, but you can't convince people that you are a viable candidate worth voting for. You were asked to talk about your latest research, but it didn't seem to go well. All of those are presentation opportunities, and with the right techniques, you have a far better chance of success.

Presentations are everywhere. You may think they just happen at conferences, but any time you have to inform, persuade, or entertain even one other person, you could be doing a presentation. Experienced presenters and speakers make it look easy, but there are so many presentations that fail for lack of simple techniques, or failure to acquire basic skills. The aim of this book is to lift your skill level, wherever you might be on the scale.

*Don't Show Your Underware* is an essential, practical guide to presentations. Whether you're a beginner or an experienced professional, you'll find this reference guide packed with practical hints and tips covering every facet of modern presentations.

There are already many books about presentations and public speaking, but most focus predominantly, or only, on speaking. Today's business executives, professionals, trainers and educators are increasingly required to present information that involves pictorial information such as statistics and graphs, sales and organizational charts, flow charts, hierarchies, processes etc., as well as formats including computer data, video and increasingly, multimedia. Whatever your situation you'll find help here.

**What Is a Presentation?**

There are many definitions of "presentation," but for the purpose of this book, a presentation is a "communication with a purpose."

The purpose includes informing, persuading, explaining, and raising questions. The audience might be a single person, or an audience of hundreds or thousands. Presenting to even one person can be daunting, and this book aims to provide practicable advice for a wide range of presentation situations. It covers the planning stages, and the practicalities of delivery.

What this book doesn't do is set out a single method or formula for presentation success. Most books on the topic of presentation suggest a specific approach or set of techniques. Or they put forward 7 simple tips, or 19 unforgettable secrets. By contrast, this book recognizes that what works for me might not work for you. If your natural style is to move about when presenting, don't try to force yourself to stand still behind a lectern. Instead, harness your movement to punctuate a point or introduce a new one. If your natural preference is to stay still, don't force yourself to move around the stage, but try to introduce a few carefully selected gestures to bring a little life into your presentation.

Speaking involves only one of our receptive senses — hearing — but experience tells us that we don't remember too much of what we hear. Science confirms that little more than 10% of our information is received through hearing, while around 75% is received visually. Most of us remember much more of what we see than what we hear. Take a moment to think back to the last party, meeting, or presentation you attended. You can probably remember much more of what you saw than of what you heard.

Presentations, as distinct from straightforward speeches, use visual as well as audio communication. They also frequently use techniques such as props, demonstrations, interactive audience participation, humor, entertainment, drama and a range of other techniques explained in this reference book. Speeches are often aimed simply at providing information to the audience. Political speeches might also try to inspire confidence, calm fears, or call the party faithful to action. Presentations also have specific aims. As a presenter you have to know your purpose, devise a strategy to achieve it, deliver the presentation, and check that it has succeeded.

This doesn't mean that giving presentations is just for the professionals. Far from it. The tips and techniques outlined in this book are relevant to a wide range of presentation situations such as staff meetings, presenting reports and proposals at work, training courses and workshops, addresses to seminars and conferences, sales presentations, product launches, or professionals on the speaker circuit. Even to general conversation.

In this book the presenter is the central character and has the key role. If you wish to design a multimedia presentation that does all the work and you simply switch it on and off, then this is the wrong book for you. A multimedia presentation is more like a TV program, and although there is much here that will help, you should really be consulting books more specifically on television and multimedia production, especially for the technicalities of these media.

Because you are central to the presentation, you are also central to this book, and so it includes the basics of good communication and public speaking techniques. The best technology cannot compensate for a presentation that is poorly structured, not relevant to the audience, over-long or poorly delivered. In presentation as in most other fields of human endeavor, good technique is fundamental. Presentation aids are no substitute for good content and technique; they are tools to enhance and improve your presentations, and help ensure that you achieve your purpose.

The medium should never become the message. Used well, modern presentation aids can add effectiveness, hold audience attention, increase retention, ensure that you meet your objective, and make you look more professional. (And maybe get you invited to do it again!)

This is not the kind of book that should be read from cover to cover. Instead you should dip into what you need when you need it. There are numerous suggestions for the various steps and stages of planning, preparing and delivering presentations, as well as diagrams such as common audience seating arrangements. The Summary of Hints and Tips (Chapter 10) is cross-referenced to the sections where they are dealt with in more detail. This book is designed as a practical reference to keep handy and use whenever you need to give a successful presentation.

As far as possible, this handbook is up to date with modern presentation aids and technology. Simple, practical explanations are given to guide presenters through equipment and facilities such as reverse projection, computer-generated slides, data projection, teleprompters, remote slide changers, and more.

There are checklists that offer guidance, and Chapter 9 is a worked example so you can see the steps taken to develop and deliver a specific presentation. You might use that as a model, or adapt it to suit your own specific aims and circumstances.

### What Is Underware?

Underware is simply any part of a presentation experience that the audience should not see. It includes that desktop screen, the presenter standing in front of a screen to point to part of a projected image, a prop in full view before it is needed, and even the presenter's notes. When you looked at the cover of this book, didn't you linger for a moment, wondering what all these files and folders were? When a presenter shows you the desktop instead of the title slide of the presentation, don't you wonder about those too? Which means you are immediately distracted from the purpose of the presentation, because the presenter showed you something you shouldn't see — underware. See also Appendix D.

### Presentation Horror Stories

Throughout the book, you'll find presentation horror stories. All of these I have witnessed, or done. The ones I've done — I've tried to do only once. Many of the ones I have seen, I've seen more than once. Some are tales of the individual presenter — some involve group presentations usually in a workshop setting. We've all seen them. That's the problem. There are so many poor presentations that it is easy to bring examples to mind. Each one illustrates a problem that undermined the purpose of the presentation. I include them as (anonymous but real) learning points.

# ❶
# Defining Your Purpose

*Purpose – Any presentation has a purpose, and the planning, preparation and performance depends on knowing that purpose, and aiming to achieve it.*

## 1.1 CREATING INSTANT PRESENTATIONS

If you want this book in a nutshell, this is it.

Here's a scenario. Your boss walks in and tells you that the vice president of the company has arrived, and that in 10 minutes, you have to do a presentation on that important development you've been working on. How do you set about it?

It's easier than you think. The first rule is — don't panic. It's counterproductive, and you don't have time. Leave any panicking till later.

Instead, be flattered that you have been asked. Consider it as a big vote of confidence in you. Others might have been asked, but you were chosen. Revel in it, and use the adrenalin rush.

**Purpose**

First, what is the purpose of the presentation. Are you being asked to explain something? Describe something? Persuade people?

**Title Selection**

Now, pick your title. For this purpose all you need to do is make your title into a question, a challenge, or a judgment.

Don't settle for:
"Our new development "
- That would suggest a descriptive or narrative account
- Doesn't suggest a structure or conclusion

Instead, try:
"What is this new development?"
OR "What will we gain from this new development?"
OR "Why this new development is vital to us?"

Any of these will
- allow your enthusiasm to come into play
- suggest a structure and conclusion
- invite your audience to become involved

**Conclusion**

Write this when you've settled on the title. Decide what you want your audience to know or learn, or what question you want them to consider. For example, what are the two main things that are new about this development, or the gain from it, or the two main reasons why it is vital to us? Just like a high school or college essay, a good choice of title suggests the form of a conclusion, and implies a pathway toward that conclusion. With 10 minutes to prepare, this is as fast a technique as you'll find.

**Parts 1 and 2**

Having "anchored" the presentation with a title and conclusion, you now have to develop the body of the presentation. Part 1 is the first thing you want people to know about the new development and part 2 is the second. (Given time, you might go to 3.)

For example if teamwork and greater efficiency are the two elements of the new development, it shouldn't be difficult to pick an illustration of each. If improved quality and lower costs are the reasons why it is vital, you should be able to offer some brief examples.

**Introduction**

This is written last. It's the bit where you tell them what you're going to tell them, and now that you know what you're going to tell them, you can scribble it down.

For example, you might need notes that allow you to stand up and say:

*"Good evening colleagues. I think we can expect two clear gains from this new development. One is in increased efficiency, and the other is in market development. Let me explain."*

OR

*"Good evening. Sailing is my passion, and I want to share with you a couple reasons why I love it so much. The first is about the competition of sailing, and the second is the teamwork involved."*

### General Points

Try to include some form of visual aid. You may not have time to do much by way of preparing aids, so look around to see if anything within the room or general area (including people) can serve to illustrate a point.

### Examples

Use the people to illustrate statistics. Everyone stands up. Have 4 of every 5 sit down to illustrate an 80% level of customer satisfaction, and ask what has to be done to satisfy the remainder i.e., those still standing.

Arrange a few colleagues in race boat positions and point out the duties and responsibilities of each in turn.

Cut up a cucumber or banana from the hotel kitchen, or tear up a newspaper page to illustrate market share or other statistics. I once saw a presenter take an old phone book, and try to rip it up to illustrate a tipping point — the force needed to start the tear.

*Remember to:*

| | |
|---|---|
| Tell them what you're going to tell them | (Introduction) |
| Tell them | (Parts 1 and 2) |
| Tell them what you've told them | (Conclusion) |

Now wasn't that easier than you thought it would be?

## 1.2 WHY YOU?

You might think you never have to do presentations, but when you think about it, you'll realize that you do. In this world of hardware and software, you are the essential liveware. Maybe formal presentations are not going to be a regular part of your working life, but any time you have to persuade, inform, or discuss with even one person, you're presenting.

One of the commonest fears is that of standing up and presenting to an audience. Survey after survey shows that people are more afraid of that than of death! I doubt that finding, but I have seen enough people either refusing, or becoming extremely nervous at the prospect. All too often their nervousness is carried over into the presentation, which does less well than they'd like, which in turn adds to that nervousness in a vicious cycle of negative feedback.

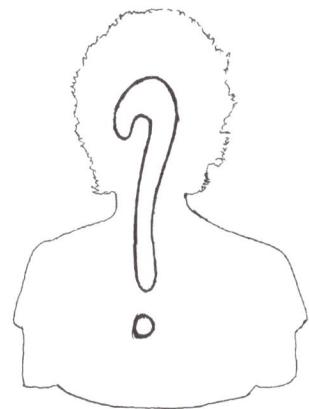

*Figure 1. Why You?*

Those people have not realized something.

Being asked (or instructed) to do a presentation is a not a punishment. You are being recognized as the person with the experience or knowledge that is needed. You are being given a vote of confidence. Carry that confidence into your presentation, and use its success to generate a cycle of positive feedback. Each presentation you do will be easier and better than the one before.

**Why Are You Doing This Presentation?**

First, it's important to understand that you may not always be the best person to undertake a specific presentation. If you feel it is beyond your remit, your area of expertise or your capabilities, be prepared to say so, and argue your case if necessary.

Assuming you are the right person, let's consider a few scenarios. It might be a college presentation as part of your coursework, part of a job application process, a work-based presentation on a new idea or development, or a presentation to shareholders, or other group. For each of these, you will have a specific purpose in mind.

| *Presentation* | *Your Purpose* |
|---|---|
| College presentation | Achieve best grade |
| Job application | Get the job |
| New idea or development | Have the idea understood and accepted |
| Shareholders meeting | Have your annual report adopted |
| Zoning board | Have your case accepted |
| Sales pitch | Clinch the sale |
| Sales pitch | Start a speaking career |

Whatever the presentation, having a clear idea of why you are doing it will help you to design it, and help maintain your motivation. You might find it interesting to consider the purpose of any presentation in the context of the triangular graph below.

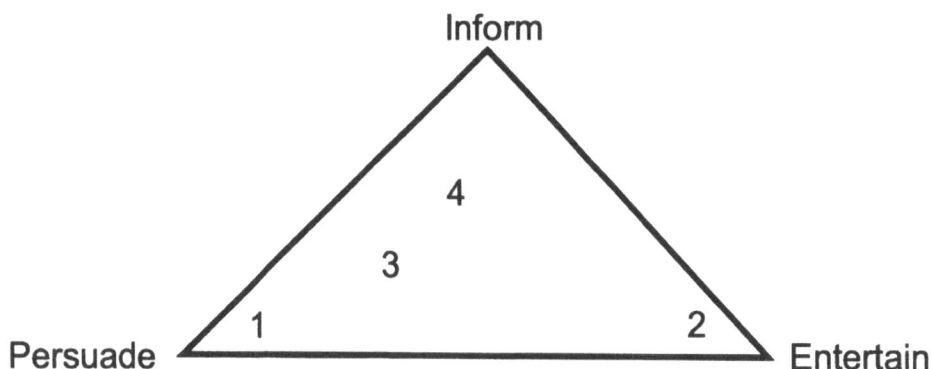

*Figure 2. Presentation purposes*

1. Sales presentation. There will be some information, and perhaps some entertainment, but the purpose is to persuade people to buy
2. After-dinner speech. Although some information may be provided, the main purpose is to entertain.
3. Political speech. Perhaps a little entertainment, and some information, but these usually lean heavily towards persuasion.
4. Conference Keynote Speech. Some entertainment, some persuasion, but the purpose is mainly to inform.

For any presentation you are trying to design, what is your chief purpose, and what will best help you to achieve it?

**Timing. How long do you have?**

First, what preparation time do you have? If this is an "instant presentation'" — go back to Chapter 1.1 right now. If you have preparation time, make sure it is enough, and decide how best to use it. What is the time allocation for the presentation? You may be able to decide how long you need, but more usually you'll be given a timescale to work to. Knowing your word count/ speaking speed will help, and remember to allow time for people to read and absorb any graphics, especially maps or charts that you plan to use.

**Venue. Where will you be presenting?**

It helps if you know where you'll be working. If you don't, try to find out so that you can reduce the number of unknowns (lighting, ambient noise, potential seating layout, etc.).

**Audience. Who are they?**

It isn't easy to do a presentation to an unknown group, but usually you know something about your audience. The more you know, the more likely you are to be able to tailor your presentation to them, and so achieve your purpose.

Let's take a closer look at this. If your presentation is part of your college coursework, and the purpose is to achieve the best grade, then it's unlikely that a jokey presentation with few facts or serious discussion points is going to do the job. In other situations, some self-deprecating humor can work to get the audience on your side. For a job application, you need to paint a positive picture of your accomplishments, and be able to back those up with references, and other data. Management will probably need hard data, especially financial information, to convince them that a new idea is worthwhile. Selling yourself as a client to new customers is difficult, and you have to focus on what they need, and to which of their problems you are the answer.

| *Presentation* | *Likely Audience* |
|---|---|
| College presentation | College staff |
| Job application | Employer, Human Resources staff |
| New idea or development | Management and/or colleagues |
| Zoning board | Zoning board members |
| Sales pitch | New or existing clients |

### The Right Pitch

A presenter has to be seen to be knowledgeable. A professional audience will expect professional vocabulary. A public audience can reasonably be expected to need explanation of some technical terms that a professional audience would not. A young audience is more likely to understand some modern slang that would be less familiar to an older audience.

### Structure

Every good story has a start, a middle, and an end. Here's an example.

| Tell them what you're going to tell them. | I'll give you three good reasons why we should parachute out of this plane. |
|---|---|
| Tell them. | First, the engines are on fire.<br>Second, we're just about out of fuel.<br>Third, in three minutes we'll fly into that mountainside. |
| Tell them what you've told them. | So that's three good reasons why we should jump – NOW! |

*TABLE 1. STORY STRUCTURE*

*Planning and preparation are dealt with more fully in 2.2*

## 1.3 WORKING WITH STATEMENT TITLES

### The First Step

If there's a key step in the planning process, it's picking a good title. Get the title right, and everything else falls into place. The corollary of that is that if you're looking at a title and not sure how to continue, it's probably because you have the wrong title. (Think back. Didn't your teachers at high school or college tell you the same thing about writing essays?)

Should you be planning a career as a speaker, you might be thinking of basing it on a specific area of expertise. Perhaps you are an expert on, for example, goal setting. If so, try using the techniques below on that topic.

The right title is one that will point the way. Let's see what that means in practice.

### Statement Titles

Take a business topic such as "Internal Communications." While it may be a reasonable topic, it doesn't really work as a title. Try it. Write it at the top of a page, and see what you can come up with. (If you don't know anything about internal communications, pick any topic about which you are knowledgeable.)

I suspect that you had no difficulty in writing down a number of headings, and perhaps you were even able to assemble them into some sequence. Even so, this isn't an easy exercise, and the biggest difficulty is deciding on how to close.

Defining Your Purpose

"So that's what I think about Internal Communications."

Doesn't that sound weak?

The title can be improved on by limiting it.

"The Five Most Important Elements of Internal Communications."

Now we have more guidance on how to continue. From all that we know about Internal Communications, we have to select the five most important, and we can arrange them in ascending or descending order. For each, we need to explain why it is important. The conclusion is also easy.

"I'm sure you'll agree that these are The Five Most Important Elements of Internal Communications."

That's what I mean about the right title pointing the way. If you have a title that is a statement you can always improve it by this process. Some examples:

| Topic | Title |
|---|---|
| Sailing | The five things I enjoy most about sailing |
| Digital photography | Four advantages of digital photography |
| Interpersonal skills | The three most crucial interpersonal skills |

### Title

The introduction's job is to tell them what you're going to tell them. Your introduction has to get the audience's attention, especially if they are restless after a break or a previous, less interesting presentation. First you have to introduce the topic and show the topic's importance. Next present your title, and list the main headings you'll be using. This is called the "route map" or "presentation path."

### Conclusion

The conclusion's job is to tell them what you've told them. It signals to the audience that you'll be finished soon, but what is more important is that it should summarize the main ideas, and leave people with a key idea to remember.

Now we have a title, and a conclusion, but the material in between needs some organization. Sometimes that can be easy. "The Five Most Important Elements of Internal Communications" suggests the possibility of working from small scale to large, e.g., from memos to the company newsletter. "Four steps towards improved customer relations" implies an order because there is a sequence in customer relations from first contact, to contracting, to after-sales care.

If the material doesn't naturally suggest an arrangement, you have to look for one. Some possibilities are explored in Section 2.2.

Although this simple step helps with the planning, we can do better. The problem is that such a title isn't too inspiring for the audience unless they happen to be enthusiasts, and how many enthusiasts do you think there are for "Internal Communications"? Titles such as these suggest a narrative or descriptive account, and imply a passive role for the audience as recipients of information. If you are thinking of your own area of expertise, have you found a workable title?

## 1.4 PICKING BETTER TITLES

**A more useful technique is to make your title into a question, a challenge, or a judgment.**

Using this technique, as suggested in 1.1, makes planning much easier, so it's a good habit to develop. Note that the distinction between these three isn't always clear — a question might also be a challenge. For your planning purpose it really doesn't matter which you call it, so don't spend time agonizing about the category. One of the biggest advantages is that you immediately involve the audience. They want an answer to your question, want to meet your challenge, want to test your judgment. The second big advantage is that you also have a good, strong opening statement.

### Some Illustrations
*Topic: Internal Communications*

| | |
|---|---|
| *How good are our internal communications?* | *(Question)* |
| *Do we have the best internal communications?* | *(Challenge)* |
| *Our internal communication could be improved.* | *(Judgment)* |

*Topic: Sailing*

| | |
|---|---|
| *What is meant by the joy of sailing?* | *(Q)* |
| *What is so good about sailing?* | *(C)* |
| *You would enjoy sailing.* | *(J)* |

*Topic: Evaluating Our Business*

| | |
|---|---|
| *What is the value of our business?* | *(Q)* |
| *Can we increase the value of our business?* | *(C)* |
| *Is the value of our business high enough?* | *(J)* |

Titles such as these are much easier to plan, because you have clear guidance to the conclusion, and to how you should get there.

Let's go back to the title we used earlier — "How Good Are Our Internal Communications?"

The conclusion has to be an answer to that question such as good, average or poor. To reach that conclusion you have to provide supporting evidence. You can decide how much evidence, prioritize it, and develop each heading according to how much time you have, how important the topic is, how important a decision has to be made, etc.

Since this is such an important point, let's work on one of the following examples.

**Topic: Evaluating our business.**
(This should have automatic appeal to owners, management and employees.)

**Title: What is the value of our business?**

**Conclusion: We have a financial value of $X, a community value that is high, a moderate environmental value, and a high social value.**

Defining Your Purpose

To reach this conclusion we have to provide the evidence.

The **financial value** is a matter of numbers, and should be reasonably straightforward.

The **community value** might be assessed through local charitable donations, liaison with local education, or other support that the business provides.

The **environmental value** could be the effect on local air or water quality, traffic volumes, noise, etc.

The **social value** could be the contribution to local employment, or the satisfaction levels among employees, customers, suppliers, etc.

Now we can write the introduction.

"Today I want to answer the question, 'What is the value of our business?'. I'll be looking at four main elements of our value — the familiar financial value, but also our community value, environmental value, and the social value to the people who work with us as colleagues, customers and suppliers."

Get the right title and planning is made easier, and your presentation falls into place.

Posing a question has other distinct advantages. First, it's more likely to allow your enthusiasm to come into play, since you can select the most important issues or elements. Second, and perhaps more important, it invites your audience to become involved. Even if they are not too enthusiastic about "internal communications" — they may be enthusiastic about how to improve them or about any cost savings or greater efficiencies that arise from them.

Think back to any presentations you've seen, or had to do.

*How many had questions as the title?*
*Might the others have been more interesting if they had?*
*Would they have involved the audience if they had?*
*Would they have been easier to plan?*
*Which would you prefer to plan and deliver?*

To see a fully developed example of a presentation using this technique, go to Chapter 9.

## 1.5 MEETING AUDIENCE EXPECTATIONS

**Any audience has expectations.**
**Why are they here?**
**Does your audience expect to be informed of something?**
**Are they here to be persuaded?**
**Is entertainment important?**

**Stand up to entertain an audience that expects information, and you are unlikely to be any better received than the after-dinner speaker who stands up only to inform.**

**Why?**

When first asked to do a presentation, "Why" is one of the questions you need to ask. A good way to make sure that you meet audience expectations is to agree on a title or topic at an early stage. As shown in Chapter 1.4, it can be useful to have a title that poses a question, issues a challenge, or tests a judgment.

Spending time to make sure that you have the right title is time well spent. It helps to make sure that you are meeting those audience expectations, and achieving your purpose.

When you stand up, you have to show confidence in what you are doing. You may not be confident in the outcome, especially if you are presenting a challenge or judgment that may not carry the day, but that is a separate issue. You audience needs to see someone who has planned their presentation and delivers it competently and confidently. The more presentations you do, the more competent and self-confident you will become.

On conclusion, be sure to thank your audience for their attention, or their time. Finishing on a positive note is not only polite, but helps to leave a good impression.

Indicate your availability. Perhaps that is already decided for you by a higher layer of management, or by the organizers of an event.

If you're an independent presenter or speaker, you're there to provide a total package of service and after-care. You can stay behind should anyone wish to talk to you. You'll be able to answer other questions over coffee. Have business cards available for follow up. Invite people to write questions on the back of their business card and have a clearly labeled jar or box in which to collect them. Make sure that any questions that you collect are answered.

# ❷
# Preliminary

*Preliminary – the early stages of planning.*

## 2.1 THE PRESENTATION HIERARCHY

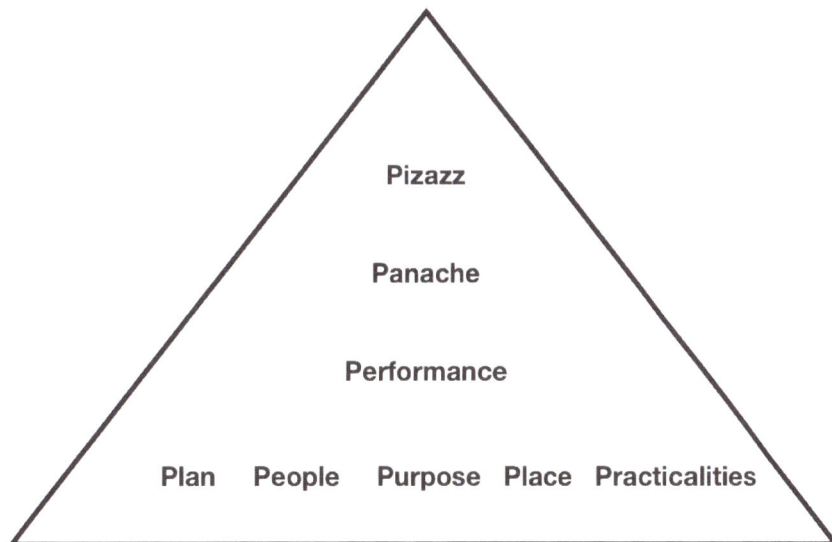

Pizazz

Panache

Performance

Plan　　People　　Purpose　　Place　　Practicalities

*Figure 3. Presentation Hierarchy*

For any presentation, the central foundation piece is the purpose. Without that purpose, you can't begin to design a presentation. To one side, planning will depend on the audience to whom you intend to present. To the other, the place where the presentation will happen, and other practicalities (such as the time and facilities available) will come into play.

Once you know the purpose, and you know who your audience will be, you can plan, taking into account whether it's a small meeting room or an auditorium, and practicalities such as the time of day, the facilities available, whether this is a freestanding event or a component of large one, etc. The performance you design and deliver will depend on having all of those foundation pieces firmly in place. A change to any of those foundation pieces is likely to change what you do, even if only slightly.

With practice, develop some panache to improve your delivery.

Top it off with some pizazz to make it memorable.

Sounds easy, but like any other skill, it requires work (preparation) and practice.

Think of music. Many of us can achieve some basic skills, but it takes more practice to achieve mastery. With mastery of an instrument comes the ability to add panache and pizazz to your performance.

Don't think of any of these stages in terms of specific skills.

Your situation, and the purposes you need to fulfill may require mastery of a limited set of skills. For you, panache and pizazz have to be seen in relation to that skill set. For someone aiming to be a professional presenter, the skill set will be much broader, and panache and pizazz will be set against that larger skill set and greater proficiency.

What do you see as essential basic presentation skills that you need to master in your own context and for your own purposes? A first step in your development as a presenter would be to master these.

The next step would be to identify those skills or techniques that you regard as adding panache or pizazz to your basic set.

Once you've done that, you'll likely find that in doing so, you've expanded your basic skills. Your definitions of panache and pizazz will also move up, and so your development as a presenter is underway.

Only you can set a limit on that development, and the aim of this book is to help you raise that limit.

An alternative way of thinking about presentations is to think of the purpose as being supported by a three-legged stool. The three legs of the stool are: *Environment, Eloquence or Expression, Execution*

**Environment is about the audience — are they comfortable, warm or cold, able to see, able to hear, etc.?**

**Eloquence/Expression is about you and your title selection, arguments, points of discussion, etc.**

**Execution is about your selection and use of words, images, props, etc.**

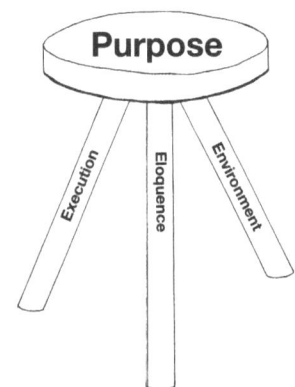

*Figure 4. Three Legged Stool*

All three are necessary to support the purpose, but they don't necessarily need to be equal to do the job. Sometimes one might be more important than the other two, but if any of them are missing, the stool falls over and cannot support the purpose. I find it useful from time to time to remind myself of the three-legged stool.

## 2.2 CHOOSING AN APPROACH

Your purpose and title will often suggest an appropriate approach as you consider the task ahead.

**Step 1. Which approach will work best?**

*Topical:* A current issue or challenge faced by the organization. One heading seems naturally to precede another. It's one of the most common types of arrangements, and it is especially useful for informative and entertaining speeches.

*Titles*

> Are we ready for the upturn in the economy?
> Are we investing enough in technology?
> Is our staff training program sufficient to keep us ahead of the competition?

*Chronological:* This arrangement is useful in informative and persuasive speeches, both of which require background information. For example, the sequence of events from design to production to sale, stages in a process, milestones in a history, key moments, critical points in a pathway.

*Titles*

> What were the key steps in our successful bid?
> What led us to this situation?

*Place:* Organizes material according to location. For example consider 'Customer Relations' starting with the effect of advertising, then contact with the sales force, calls to the sales office, and after sales service. Usually best if you work from the local to the distant.

*Titles*

> Where are our clients?
> Where are our suppliers?
> Where are the key components of our supply chain?

*Classification:* Puts things into categories. You can use this pattern for all three speech purposes.
*Titles*

> Who are our customers?
> Who are our suppliers?
> What are our best sellers?

*Problem/Solution:* Outline a problem, review options, and select an answer. Also useful in persuasive presentations. First describe the cause of a problem, or the reason for a suggestion, then describe its effect. For example, poor quality control leading to customer dissatisfaction, adverse publicity and a sales slump.

> *Titles*
> Why are our sales on a downward trend?
> Why are our costs rising?
> Who now are our typical customers?

*Cause/Effect:* Identify effect (which may be good or bad), review factors which affect it, select key causes (using quantitative or qualitative indicators as appropriate). For example, poor quality control leading to customer dissatisfaction, adverse publicity and a sales slump.

> *Titles*
> Do good presentations boost sales?
> Do poor presentations lose sales?
> Do production delays affect sales?

## Step 2. Define the conclusion

| *Title* | *Conclusion* |
|---|---|
| Are we ready for the upturn in the economy? | Yes, we are. |
| Are we investing enough in technology? | No, we are not. |
| Who are our customers? | Local businesses. |
| Why are our costs rising? | Insufficient monitoring. |
| Do poor presentations lose sales? | Yes they do. |

## Step 3. Select the three or four main points

*Examples:*

We are ready for the upturn in the economy because we have
- a strong product line
- an effective staff
- a loyal customer base

Our customers are
- mainly businesses in the local service sector
- mostly long-term customers
- hardly any of the new businesses starting in the area

Our costs rise because
- we have too many people spending
- we allow them to spend too much
- we don't monitor what they spend it on

Poor presentations lose sales because
- people lose confidence in us
- our people project a poor image of themselves and of us
- customers don't associate us with quality
- we don't give them clear information

**Step 4. Put steps 1, 2 and 3 together, and you have an outline**

For a brief presentation, this might be enough. For a longer presentation, flesh out the details. See Chapter 9 for a step-by-step example of a presentation requested, designed and delivered.

## 2.3 IDENTIFYING THE KEYSTONE FACT

Sometimes a presentation involves a keystone fact. A keystone is the wedge-shaped stone at the center of an arch. That stone locks the two sides of the arch together. Without the keystone, the arch cannot stand.

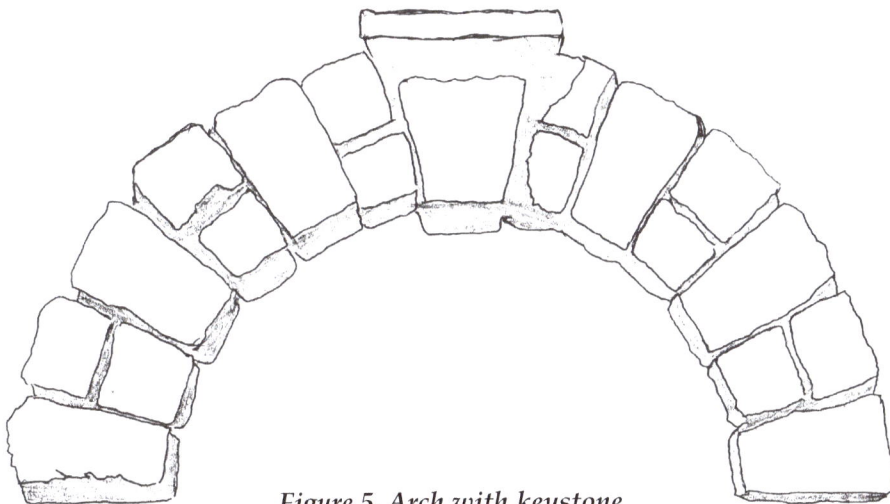

*Figure 5. Arch with keystone*

This might apply to your presentation. If so, that keystone fact needs to be prominent and reinforced by repetition.

Perhaps you are looking at internal communications because a recent snag in that area led to the loss of a major customer. That would be a keystone fact to be stated and reinforced.

A presentation on why you love sailing might have that love expressed in several ways — the feel of the wind in your face, the challenge of making the best of the wind, sounds of the wind in the rigging, the feel of the waves against the hull. The keystone fact is the love, and the elements are distributed to reinforce it.

A presentation on readiness for an upturn in the economy might be necessary because the business is not considered to be ready. Unreadiness is a keystone fact, along with the potential consequences of that unreadiness.

Not every presentation will have a keystone fact, but if you identify one, and use it, your presentation will be stronger and more successful.


## 2.4 SELECTING A TECHNIQUE

The same presentation can be delivered in a number of different ways.

Do you simply stand and deliver? Should you keep it simple with a flip chart? Do you need the power and versatility of PowerPoint, Keynote, or similar? The more you involve aids, props and technology, the more impressive it might all be, but the more there is to go wrong.

Which method will best suit the circumstances, the time available, the size and nature of your audience, the facilities available to you, your own capabilities, and most important of all, your purpose? There is no simple answer, but which do you think is better — keeping it simple and achieving your purpose, or being over elaborate and not achieving that purpose?

When people think of a presentation, they nearly always think of a talk. Sometimes, especially for a short presentation, speech may be all that is needed.


**Aids**

A little help from your friends.

Even a short presentation is likely to benefit from an aid or two. An aid is something that helps to make the point. It also takes attention away from you for a moment or two, allowing you to relax a little, or check your notes. It doesn't have to be elaborate. Gestures can be used to emphasize an upward or downward trend. With a little creativity household or office items can be used effectively. Hold up a pen to represent written communication, or an umbrella for shelter, a brush to signify sweeping change.

For a small audience, a flip chart might be useful, especially if the presentation is interactive.

For longer presentations, it can become more important to consider other techniques that will help to make your point and achieve your purpose.

Would a picture help? A photograph, a diagram, or some other pictorial representation?

Would a prop help? A model or icon to represent an idea, a point of view, etc.?

Would sound help? An interview, the noise of the shop floor, or of angry customers?

Would video help? A process, an operation, or anything that involves movement.

Would audience involvement help? Model a situation with one or more volunteers.

Carefully selected audio visual aids can make any presentation more effective.

Might PowerPoint or Keynote serve you better? Not necessarily, if for no other reason that you may not have enough time. Both are extremely powerful and versatile, especially if you follow a few simple rules, and don't get carried away by all the bells and whistles on offer. A simpler approach is Google Slides, which doesn't offer all the bells and whistles but is free, and will be perfectly adequate for many presentations.

Whichever software you use, try to obey the Rule of Seven. This says that there should be no more than seven lines of text on a slide, and no more than seven words per line. I find it works pretty well, and often leads me to take a crowded slide and redesign it into two or three slides.

These slides illustrate the point.

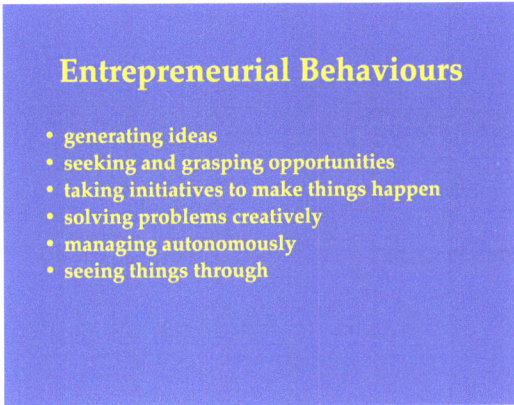

Figure 6. Entrepreneurial Behaviors

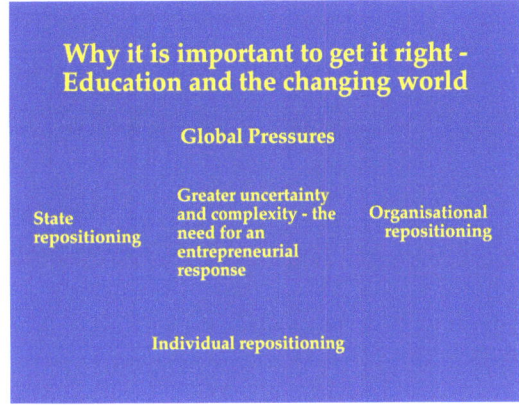

Figure 7. Getting it Right

These first two are OK. The text is clear, and large enough to read easily. Both more or less comply with the Rule of Seven.

The ones below are not. "The Essences of Owner Managed Business" is not easy to read because there is too much information. The "Open Source Defined" slide also has far too much information, and the text is too small to read easily.

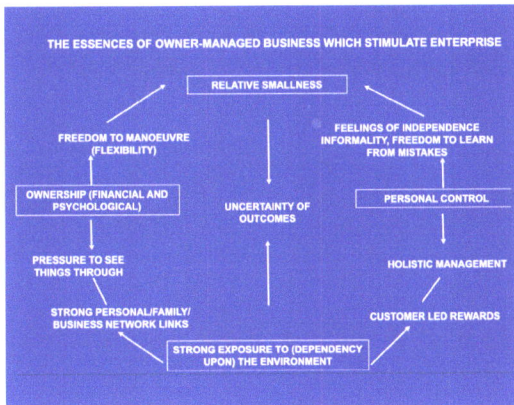

Figure 8. Owner Managed Business

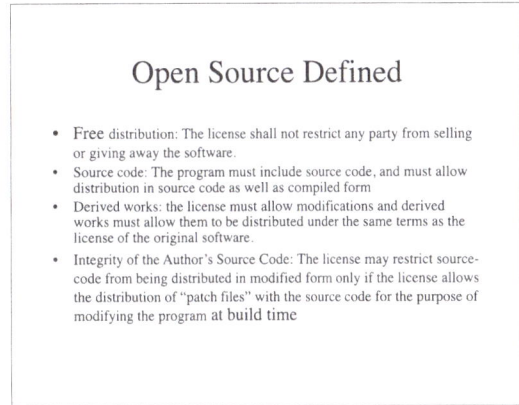

Figure 9. Open Source Defined

Figure 10, the last one, is even more crowded, and looks as though it has been taken, perhaps from a leaflet, without being redesigned as a slide.

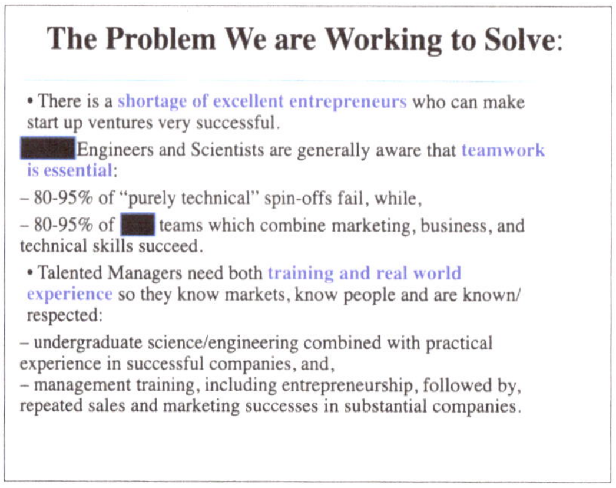

**The Problem We are Working to Solve:**

• There is a shortage of excellent entrepreneurs who can make start up ventures very successful.

▮▮▮▮ Engineers and Scientists are generally aware that teamwork is essential:

– 80-95% of "purely technical" spin-offs fail, while,

– 80-95% of ▮▮▮ teams which combine marketing, business, and technical skills succeed.

• Talented Managers need both training and real world experience so they know markets, know people and are known/respected:

– undergraduate science/engineering combined with practical experience in successful companies, and,

– management training, including entrepreneurship, followed by, repeated sales and marketing successes in substantial companies.

*Figure 10. Problem to solve*

Your task may be easier if there is a corporate style or template for you to follow, but otherwise you have control over the color and style selections for your presentation. Choose wisely, always remembering your purpose, and give your audience time to read each slide.

The horror stories scattered throughout this book are reminders that not everyone plans or prepares properly, or makes careful or appropriate selections of aids, or even of personnel to do the presentation.

## VISUAL AIDS HORROR STORY

A staff development presentation on 'Motivation' was led by a member of the management team. He arrived with a set of carefully prepared slides that he proceeded to screen. Each one was well designed and easy to read, and the presenter read aloud each one, in full, to the increasingly dismayed and decreasingly motivated audience!

PRESENTATION PURPOSE
– to improve staff motivation

THE PROBLEM
– poor delivery technique

RESULT
– purpose not achieved

SOLUTIONS
– Better planning and design
– Rehearse

## 2.5 BEING WHO YOU ARE

**Make the best of yourself**

You are a presenter, and before you are introduced, or even stand up, people will be looking at you, with curiosity, with anticipation, perhaps with bias or disinterest. It's often a good idea to assume an initial neutrality upon which you can build a positive image.

What do people see when they look at you?

Dress
Age
Gender
Body language

Your greatest asset is yourself, so you need to be fully aware of your strengths and weaknesses as a presenter. Build on your strengths and work on your weaknesses.

Use this checklist to pick out areas where you think you may have a problem:

| | | | |
|---|---|---|---|
| Height | Small | Medium | Tall |
| Voice quality | Poor | Average | Good |
| Command of language | Poor | Average | Good |
| Diction | Poor | Average | Good |
| Natural speaking pace | Fast | Medium | Slow |
| Voice modulation | Low | Average | High |
| Confidence level | Poor | Average | Good |
| Dress sense | Poor | Average | Good |
| Enthusiasm | Poor | Average | Good |

As an example, here's my own profile.

| | | | |
|---|---|---|---|
| Height | Small | **Medium** | Tall |
| Voice quality | Poor | Average | **Good** |
| Command of language | Poor | Average | **Good** |
| Diction | Poor | Average | **Good** |
| Natural speaking pace | **Fast** | Medium | Slow |
| Voice modulation | Low | **Average** | High |
| Confidence level | Poor | Average | **Good** |
| Dress sense | **Poor** | Average | Good |
| Enthusiasm | Poor | Average | **Good** |

Being of medium height means I need to be careful to make sure I can see and be seen.

My naturally fast speaking pace means I have to remember to slow down.

My confidence comes from years of experience, and from preparation.

My poor dress sense means I have to ask for and use the advice of others, but I've learned a few simple rules to help.

Enthusiasm can make or break any presentation. Don't be afraid to let a little passion come through.

Try to wear a color that contrasts with your background. If you don't know what that background will be, try strong colors.

Avoid shirts or ties that shimmer or have other visual distractions. A plain colored shirt and a contrasting tie will suffice. The contrasting tie will help focus attention on your face.

Women should generally avoid jewelry that is distracting. You want the audience to focus on you and your message, not on your sparkling necklace or jangling bangle. Long hair may also be a problem, obscuring your vision at times and risking entanglement with props, mikes, etc.

If you are going to be wearing a radio mike, please avoid shirts or blouses that are prone to static electricity. This can cause distracting and possibly even damaging noise spikes in the audio system.

At a conference, you might have a lanyard for your ID badge / ticket. I prefer to remove this for a presentation since it so easily gets in the way. Even a clip-on badge is probably better in a pocket than hanging on your shirt pocket, catching the light and offering distraction.

### Confidence

Often this is what holds people back (see 5.1). Maybe it's the fear of standing up before an audience; maybe it's being aware of a lack of skills; maybe it's something else. If you're asked to provide a presentation, isn't it a vote of confidence in you? Someone thinks you have the skills and the knowledge to do the job and achieve the purpose. Prove them right.

Are you a naturally confident person or are you more representative of the majority who are terrified by the prospect of standing up and speaking in public? Even professionals can find this terrifying, and some face it every time they go on. I have stood in the wings and watched some very experienced performers go through the routines they have developed to help them through. They walk on stage, and you'd never guess that a few moments before they were a trembling bag of nerves.

In radio studios, I've seen presenters cough and splutter as they work their vocal cords, and gather themselves as they await the moment when the red light goes on and the mike is live. A good technique that many use is to stand tall with your back against a wall, and breathe slowly and deeply. Gently shake the tension out of your arms, relax the legs by tensing them, and then release all the muscles in the toes, then the feet, ankles, calves and so on up to the body.

Physiologically, anxiety means your body is preparing for the "fight or flight" situation. Your heart rate goes up, trying to get more oxygen to the muscles and brain, so you may feel restless or twitchy. You may also experience an adrenalin rush as part of the same process. Many whose jobs or hobbies make this a familiar scenario will tell you that you can recognize it in yourself, and put it to good use. The athlete can use it to run faster or farther, the soldier to reach cover more quickly, the mountaineer to hang on beyond the point where he thought he could, and the presenter to think more quickly and clearly.

Recognizing it means you have to compensate for it. You will tend to talk more quickly. Your voice pitch may go up a little, so you need to make an effort to slow down, and get back to normal. You may find it more difficult than usual to hold your hand steady so avoid directing a laser pointer too early. If necessary, lean an elbow on the lectern or table to steady your arm, or rest the pointer on a blob of Blu Tack on a desk. You may find that you can't walk too steadily, so avoid walking around until later on when you may feel more relaxed. You may even find it hard to stand still, and having a lectern or podium to hold on to is useful.

Confidence can be built. Do your homework, start your planning early, rehearse the presentation, and keep it simple. Many a presentation starts with the presenter confessing nervousness, and that usually gets audience sympathy, especially if they know this is your first effort, or something you do rarely — after all most of them wouldn't be comfortable up there either. Don't overplay the card. The audience has limits to their patience and understanding. For a regular presenter, it's usually a nonstarter.

### Personality

As much as anything else, your personality will come through in your presentation style, and it should. Nothing will fail more surely than a contrived performance which is completely out of character. If you are a linear thinker and detail oriented, that will come through in your planning and delivery. It might be a problem if it limits your ability to react to sudden changes of timing or other circumstances, but your detailed planning probably includes provision for that. If you are a more relaxed person, able to work to a basic outline but capable of reacting to change, that will be clear to your audience. I am more the relaxed type than the linear, and I can readily adjust to change, but working to a strict plan is not too comfortable. Equally uncomfortable is the linear thinker who tries to be relaxed and to improvise.

The message here is not that you need to classify yourself and operate accordingly. You know yourself. You know what you are comfortable doing. Don't set that aside and try to be something different. Instead, pick out from these pages the things that you feel comfortable with and that you think you can do. As you gain experience, your comfort zone will expand, allowing you to develop additional skills, but build them on who you are. You might start by assessing your existing presentation skills using the technique outlined next, and in Appendix B.

### Knowledge

Whatever the purpose of your presentation, a certain amount of knowledge is required. Perhaps you have that already, as part of your job or hobby. Perhaps you need to acquire it in a hurry. Either way, a key skill of the presenter is to take a body of knowledge and present it in such a way that a specific audience can understand it. Sometimes that is itself the purpose of the presentation. Sometimes gaining some knowledge is a crucial step toward the purpose of persuasion, or of a decision. Fortunately there are many techniques to help you do that, and you probably already have your own favorite learning technique.

Here's another approach.

### How good am I at presentations?

Rate yourself from one to four. One is the least that is acceptable to you, and four is the best that you think you might achieve. Having written those, now write in two levels between. Most often, you'll find yourself at level two or three, sometimes at four, but hardly ever at one. Note that this is personal to you. The least that is acceptable to you is not necessarily what would apply to anyone else. This approach is intended to allow you to identify your own standards, and suggest where you need improvement.

Does any part of the example below ring true for you?

*Four: I feel confident that when asked to do a presentation, I can design and deliver it on time and achieve its purpose.*

*Three: I can design and deliver a presentation with a little difficulty and usually achieve its purpose.*

*Two: I have to work hard to design a presentation, don't always deliver it fluently, and don't always achieve the purpose.*

*One: I struggle to design and deliver presentations, and am not sure that I achieve its purpose often enough.*

Now the useful part. If you rate yourself at one, two or three, what do you need to do to move up at least one level? What resources might you need to achieve that move, and what timescale might apply?

Next, an example based on one element of the presentation process.

### How good am I at planning a presentation?

*Four: I can quickly and easily develop a full plan for most presentations I am likely to be asked to do.*

*Three: I can, given time, develop a full plan for the majority of the presentations I am likely to be asked to do.*

*Two: I need time to develop a plan for any presentation, and so I do fewer than I might.*

*One: I struggle to develop a plan for any presentation, and this limits both my confidence, and the number of presentations I feel comfortable doing.*

If you take this approach for several elements of presentation, you can identify which are your weaknesses, prioritize them, and set about addressing them using this book.

See Appendix B for another example, and Appendix C for a list of some elements you could consider.


## 2.6 FINDING YOUR VOICE

*"Is sloppiness in speech caused by ignorance or apathy? I don't know
and I don't care." – William Safire (1929-2009)*

In any presentation, the voice is an essential tool. Is your voice powerful or weak? Can you talk to a room of 30 people so that all can hear you comfortably? Do you need some help from amplification or a sound reinforcement system? In a large auditorium, a powerful voice needs to back away from a microphone (look at how far back an operatic soprano will stand from any mike), while a weaker voice is more likely to benefit from amplification, and needs to talk a little closer (but not too close) to the mike. Watch the US president at the lectern in a press conference and see that he stands upright, with the mikes down low.

Is your normal voice monotonous or does it leap to highs and lows? Either end of the scale can be equally difficult for the audience, but a confidential point can be made by lowering the voice. An emphatic point needs to be made with vocal emphasis, and pauses give people time to think; and can help to gather attention before an important point is made.

Is your voice high-pitched or low? A lower voice tends to be more comfortable to listen to, so try to keep it low if you can. Nervousness tends to make people speak a little higher than usual, so a conscious effort is probably needed to keep that voice low.

Do you speak quickly or slowly? Fast speech can be difficult for a large group to hear, so try to slow it down. Really slow speech can be irritating too. For news radio, a standard word rate is around 180 per minute, but for a presentation, you may need to be slower — 160 or 150 words per minute. A ten-minute presentation would therefore need around 1500 words. It's easy to time yourself, and calculate a comfortable pace.

Do you have any speech impediments? These you probably know about and compensate for. If you lisp, it makes sense to minimize the number of words you use with 's' sounds, and if you pronounce 'r' as 'w', you probably already avoid regular recurrences of rounded sounds. You can't eliminate such things, but there is as little point in trying too hard to evade the difficulty as there is in trying too little.

Do you have an accent? I do, and when people tell me "You have an accent," my reply is nearly always the same. "So do you." Your audience may be used to you, but not every audience will recognize some dialect words, phrases or sentence constructions that you might commonly use. Depending on the situation, you might be able to capitalize on that, but more usually you have to stick to a more readily understandable style of speech if you are to achieve your purpose.

Do you have any speech mannerisms? A difficult question, because you don't always notice these. For example, do you…

*End sentences with "you know"*
*Use the word "like" as a verbal comma*
*Sniff after each sentence*
*Start each sentence with "well," "so," or "right"*
*End each sentence on a rising note, making it sound like a question*

Or a host of others.

You might not really know, and the best way to find out is to record a conversation and listen to it afterwards. You might surprise yourself. Or ask your spouse — or better still, your kids. They can be brutally honest, but you need to know. Don't plan to purge your presentation of these mannerisms. They are part of you, and losing them entirely may make you sound too unnatural. Instead, plan to keep them to a minimum, so that they don't distract audience attention from your message. As with speech impediments, there is a balance to be maintained.

Pronunciation is also important. You can't afford to mispronounce the name of your host institution or its key people. Foreign names and places can be difficult, but make a genuine attempt. Also take care with any specialized language that your audience is likely to be familiar with.

I once had to speak at a meeting on the small Mediterranean island of Malta. I spent much of the day beforehand being coached by the hotel receptionist on how to say, "Malta is a beautiful island. I am delighted to be here." in Maltese. Other staff joined in so that as I wandered about, I could say the phrase and have them suggest corrections. Malta is such a small country that few outsiders bother to learn any Maltese, so later at the meeting, my two sentences in Maltese went down especially well.

Diction is tremendously important to the clarity of the spoken word. There's a simple experiment you can try to test this out. Try speaking softly to someone on the other side of a large room. If you slur your speech and don't pronounce the p and t sounds, you'll find that your listener has difficulties. Try it again with good diction, and the difficulties fall away. You can see this happen on stage. Actors will deliver a quiet line with exaggerated diction, to be sure that they are heard and understood.

In a large room or an auditorium, check the reverberation. That's the time taken for an echo to die away. Stand where you will be delivering the presentation, and clap your hands. Listen to that echo. If it dies quickly, all is well. If it takes time to fade away, you might have to slow down your delivery. This is because if you speak quickly, the echo of one word is still reverberating as the next arrives, and that can be difficult for the listener.

### Audio

Will they be able to hear you?

Think back to your high school classrooms. Your teachers made several presentations every day to groups of 20 to 30 with relative ease. Unless your voice is very soft, you should be able to be heard by a similar number of people in the same size of room, or slightly larger.

Here's a few things you can try to make sure your message is heard.

Stand tall. That means:

- *You can breathe more deeply and push out more volume*
- *Your voice is above head height, so the back row can hear you too*
- *They can all see you — it's easier to "tune in" to a speaker whose face you can see*

Speak a little more slowly than usual.

A slower delivery

- *helps people to absorb what you say*
- *counteracts any room echo*
- *gives you more time to think as you go*
- *gives time to develop eye contact with the audience*

Try to speak clearly. Good diction will
- *help your listeners to understand you*
- *create a better impression*
- *help to avoid misunderstanding*

Try to include variety.
- *avoid a monotone*
- *practice emphasis at key points*
- *practice quieter and louder*
- *practice changes of pace*

## VOICE HORROR STORY

A professional sportsman with a story of dedication and preparation as the key to success had attracted a large audience. After a glowing introduction, he began his talk, but clearly was new to the task. He had been told to speak up, and he did, but for only the first few words of each sentence. By the end of each sentence, his levels had dropped to barely audible, and the audience strained to hear before the audio onslaught of the next sentence.

### PRESENTATION PURPOSE
– to inform and motivate audience

### THE PROBLEM
– poor delivery technique

### RESULT
– audience less than fully informed or motivated

### SOLUTION
– voice coaching and practice to ensure all words are heard

## 2.7 PACING EXERCISE

Are you a naturally fast speaker? Here's a useful word count exercise. Use a timer set to one minute. Start reading it out loud and see how far through you are when the timer signals the end of your minute. The numbers are there to give you a word count so you can count forward or backwards from the nearest number when you stop.

Ready?

*This exercise aims to give you an idea of how fast you speak. A radio newsreader may reach around 180 words per minute, but in a presentation, you probably want to be a little slower — down to perhaps 150 words per minute. To some extent that depends on the room. In a large auditorium with echo, it's more important to slow down. A smaller room with little or no echo can take a slightly faster pace.*

*Knowing your word count helps you to plan. At a pace of 150 words per minute, a 10-minute presentation will need up to 1500 words, with no allowance made for time when you are silent, giving the audience time to look at graphics. A five-second pause for each of six graphics would reduce the total by some 30 words.*

*147*

*This exercise is printed with wider spacing, to make it easier for you to read. Since you are seeing it for the first time as you read it aloud, your pace could be a little slower than usual.*

*185*

*Reaching as far as this within a minute makes you a fast-paced speaker, and you may have to make a conscious effort to slow yourself down, especially at the start. You'll probably find yourself picking up pace as you go, but as people get used to you and your voice, this may not be much of a problem.*

*251*

**Is your pace what you expected?**
**Might you need to modify it a little?**

# ❸
# Planning

*Plan – An essential step toward achieving the purpose of any presentation.*

## 3.1 OUTLINING – A KEY PART OF THE DEVELOPMENT PROCESS

An outline is just that — no details, just the bare bones of the presentation as shown in 2.2 At this stage you can move things around, consider where props, visual aids etc. might be effectively included, and manage the overall shape of the presentation.

Unless you have a very good memory, notes are advised. Writing them is an integral part of the preparation, and having them there is a safeguard against the unexpected. If you use Keynote or PowerPoint, notes can be added on the presenter's view while remaining invisible to the audience. Even so additional notes may be helpful.

There are various ways of compiling an outline, and you should choose one that works for you. Whichever method you choose, make sure you write big and bold so that everything is clear and visible at a glance. Sometimes the outline can be developed into a planner for use as a prompt when you deliver the presentation. For example, if you outline on index cards, it is easy to develop the outline by adding notes to the cards. The same applies to Post-its. A planner page is a little more work since you might have to rewrite it a couple of times, and even if I develop the outline on Post-its, I prefer to use the planner page layout for delivery. I have to make sure it is only a prompt, and doesn't take too much of my attention away from the audience.

### Index Cards

A very common method is to use a set of index cards. Some use the small 3 x 5 variety, but I'd suggest the largest size you can find. They're no less manageable, and a lot easier to read.

The advantage of cards is that you can use one card per heading, so a basic presentation with an introduction, three main points and a conclusion could be done on as few as five cards. Each one can be rewritten independently, and it's easy to change the order of the main points if necessary.

At the planning stage, you can lay the cards out in sequence to get an overview of the presentation, and it's easy to move things around. The cards should be identified in sequence, and I've found it useful to number them 1 of 7, 2 of 7, etc. Some people take the top edge and draw a diagonal line across it, so that they can spot cards out of sequence, but I find a boldly written number in the top right corner works best for me.

Another system is to punch holes in a top corner and tie them together with treasury tags or a small piece of string. The ties for garbage or freezer bags are handy for this. A standard layout for each cards helps too, so that you always know where to look, and since they are small, you have the freedom to move about, notes in hand.

The disadvantage is that you either have to hold them in your hand, which restricts your ability to gesture or manage your aids, or you place them on a table, which makes them a little more difficult to read. A lectern is where they work best because they can lie on the top at a convenient angle and are closer to you than on a table, and more easily visible.

### Post-its

Large Post-it pads can be used in the same way. They don't come as large as index cards, but have the same advantages, and they are easily rearranged in whatever order you choose — on a wall, a window, a TV screen, etc. I've used a small stack of Post-it notes for presentations, and it works when I have something to stick them on, even a lectern.

### The Planner Page

I prefer this method because of its flexibility. The diagram below shows a format for a planner page that works for me, but you can adjust it to suit your own style. You can see a fully developed planner in Chapter 9.

*Title*                                      *Audience*

*Venue*                          *Date* / /                     *Start time*

| Introduction | 1st Heading | 2nd Heading | 3rd Heading | 4th Heading | Summary |
|---|---|---|---|---|---|
|  |  |  |  |  |  |

*TABLE 2. BASIC PLANNER*

At the outlining stage, I can use a different page for each section and rewrite it as often as I like. When I finalize the plan, I write it up on a single page. Since I use a Word template, I do each section as a separate file using the same template, and simply cut and paste the finished sections onto the final page. The single page has all the information I need, from title and topics to timing and aids. That works for me because I can work from the notes, glancing down to stay on track, on topic and on time, but maintaining eye contact with the audience

To hold the page I use a ring binder. This allows me to prop the page up at an angle so that whether I have a table or lectern, it stands facing me and is easy to read. To get the binder to stand up, I have a few options, as follows.

1. Punch a hole on each side and link them with a treasury tag.
2. Have a plastic cable tie that can be placed under the ring binder to hold it in place.
3. Have a piece of string and tie it to a ring, go down and under the binder and back to the ring. (Make sure it's under all your pages.)
4. Instead of string, use the lanyard from your conference badge (as in the photo below).
5. Prop the binder in place and use sticky tape to hold it there.

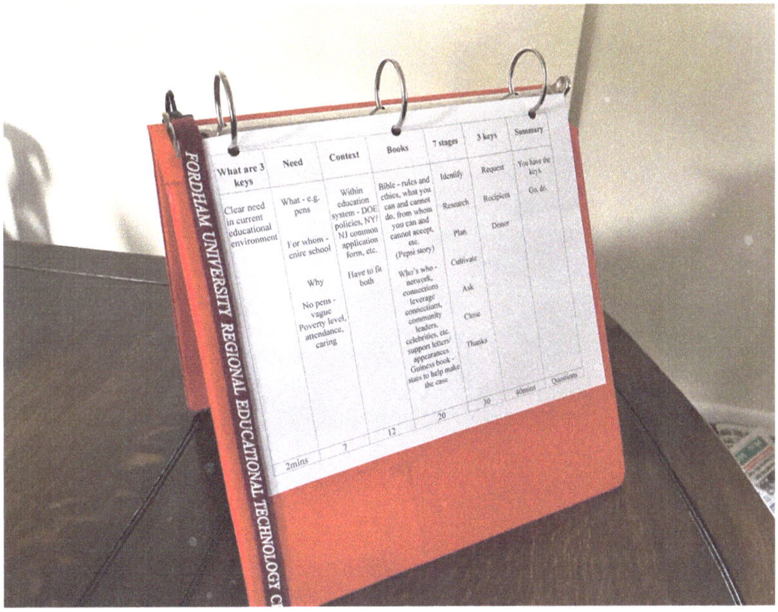

*Figure 11. Planner page on a Ring Binder*

This method gives greater flexibility to adjust the angle at which the binder stands. Since one side of the binder faces the audience, it forms a larger than usual nameplate, so I always make sure I have a large caption for them to read. My topic is an obvious caption, and if possible, I put my name there too — a little self-promotion opportunity not to be missed.

At the end you can turn over your last page to reveal a full-page size version of your business card.

The binder is also handy because it can store any other material I need — additional notes, a spare nameplate, direction to the venue, speaker agreement, invoices, fee structure, evaluation pages, spare business cards, etc.

If your budget allows, you might try a presentation folder as available from most office supply retailers. These can carry several pages, and are designed to stand on a table, as shown below.

*Figure 12. Prompt page on a Presentation Folder*

Using notes during a presentation creates some minor challenges. It is essential to number them in case you drop them, or have to go back because of a question.

I've used a treasury tag to hold notes together, and that works, but a rubber band, a twist tie and a keyring can also work. Just punch a hole in the top left corner of the cards, and tie them together.

### Notebook Planner

This is not my choice but it might be yours. Writing your plan in a notebook is OK if it's one of the large notebooks, and you can write it all on one page. I tried it once and since I had a table but no lectern, the notebook was nearly always too far away for me to read clearly, and it wasn't the type that could easily be propped up. In any case, if you can write it all on one page, the planner page works better for me. I have seen other presenters work from notebooks, sometimes successfully. If it works for you, then go ahead, but for me, while the notebook is useful for developing the plan, it isn't the best option for delivering it.

A final challenge arises with a lectern that has a mike attached to it. Usually a baseplate is fastened to the lectern, and a short gooseneck stand is added. This allows the mike to be adjusted quickly and easily, but at a cost. Paper-handling noises can be picked up by that mike, as can the noises you make picking up items (such as props, pens, laser pointers, etc.) and putting them down. Check those noise levels as part of your routine. Try to avoid putting your notes on "noisy" paper, and work on techniques for changing from one page to another as quietly as possible.

## 3.2 GATHERING AN AUDIENCE

**Who needs to know?**
**How do you reach them?**
**How do you persuade them to come?**

Sometimes presentations are ad hoc. You meet someone at work in the corridor, or they drop by your office, and suddenly the conversation becomes a presentation to an audience of one, or maybe two. Perhaps one result of this interaction might be a promotion at work, but otherwise this section is about making sure you have an audience.

Whether you're presenting as part of your job but especially as an independent presenter, promotion is involved.

Facebook (Meta) and LinkedIn are two useful social media vehicles, and there are so many others. Make sure you have a presence. Post snippets about what you do, write short articles about presentations you have done, or give some pointers. Have a look at SlideShare, where you can browse presentations sent in by others. There are several sections, including one on presentations and public speaking. Don't be overawed by the presentations already posted. Learn from them, and post your own as part of your promotion effort.

Within a company, there are opportunities to promote your presentation. One presenter I saw walked in and gave everyone a new nameplate. On the front was the name and, on the side, facing us was his topic, name and phone number. Another arranged for a cake to arrive at the coffee break preceding his presentation. The cake was lettered with his topic, which piqued everyone's curiosity and brought us to his presentation with greater anticipation than usual. Both made sure that we remembered them.

An office bulletin board can be used to remind colleagues that you will be unavailable at a particular time because you're doing a presentation. The colleague of a friend did this regularly, and trained his assistant to always mention that he "would be (or was) unavailable because he was doing a presentation." He developed a greater reputation for doing presentations than might otherwise have been the case.

Posters are often used to announce "one off" presentations, and sometimes the organizers will be happy to accept your poster design. Have a standard template available so that you can type in the title, venue, date and time as required. It doesn't cost much to print some small US letter or A4 sized posters for the organizers to distribute, and it's a legitimate advertising expense that can pay dividends. That poster may linger on a notice board long after the event, providing people with a cost-effective reminder.

Most presentations are introduced by somebody else. Sometimes the person doing this will have done their homework and be well prepared for the task, but more often you'll find that they are grateful to have some guidance from you. If nothing else, they want to be able to pronounce your name properly, especially if it's a little out of the ordinary. You'll find it useful to prepare a little introduction card or page, with brief information under the following headings:

*Title of the presentation*
*One or two reasons why it is important*
*Your qualifications as relevant to this topic*
*Your name, including a phonetic guide to pronunciation if necessary*

Don't just give the title of the presentation. Try to list some benefits to participants. Think of car sales. All modern cars can be relied on to get you where you want to go in reasonable comfort and safety. Few people buy a car on the basis of its name or the technical specifications. The car companies persuade us to buy this one or that because of the benefits of ownership — perceived status, level of comfort, reliability, fuel economy, resale value. What benefit might your audience gain from attending your presentation?

A well-organized meeting or conference will provide nameplates, but you'll find it useful to have your own with you, just in case. Print it on both faces, so that it can be read either way round. If nothing else, it means your name will be spelled correctly. Make sure the name is clear, big and bold, so that people can see it clearly. Don't just prop it on the table or lectern and expect it to stay there. Use that ever useful blob of Blu Tack (a reusable adhesive putty) or a small strip of gaffa tape to fix it in place.

Have plenty of business cards with you. If there's a convenient table near the back, lay out a fan of them, and make sure you mention that they are available. Have more with you so that as people come up to you to ask questions or make comments, you can hand them out.

Many presentations end with the presenter's contact details as the closing graphic. It's a useful ploy, but I think it is improved if it is combined with a thank you message. You're probably going to thank the audience for their attention as you close the presentation, and a visual reinforcement is entirely appropriate.

After the event, you should make it a matter of routine to send the organizers a card expressing your thanks for their assistance, inviting any comments they might have, and indicating your availability to work for them again. It'll be worth the effort to develop a template with a big, bold and eye-catching thank you (perhaps a tasteful cartoon?) that includes your contact details. Be sure to personalize every one you send.

An independent presenter has to work harder at finding the work. Most businesses agree that it is easier to attract a repeat customer than a new one. The repeat customer has had a good experience and knows and has enjoyed the product. It's generally easier to persuade such a customer to return than to entice a new customer, which is why so many businesses offer "'loyalty" rewards in one form or another.

If you find yourself doing new presentations in new venues every time, you'll be doing much preparation and research that is used only once. Coming to a familiar venue means you can spend less time on reconnaissance, and variations on a topic are easier to research, plan and prepare than a new topic. Your fee structure can recognize this and offer an appropriate incentive to rebook you.

There are agencies that can do much of this for you, and you should consider them if you intend to make a career in presentation. A speaker's bureau is one such agency, and you should investigate the local chapter of the National Speakers Association. Another useful group is Toastmasters, which offers coaching.

## 3.3 DRESSING FOR SUCCESS

Did you ever do that at high school? 'Dress for success' means that you dress to achieve the purpose. That may or may not be your own personal style, but it needn't be too much of a burden either. Let's go back to the presentation examples we used earlier (Chapter 1.2).

The thing to do is to put yourself in the mind of the audience. College staff are going to be thinking about what you say and trying to assess it for a grade. They are less likely to be concerned about your dress style, but a flamboyant or extreme appearance may distract them. A school board will probably listen more carefully to someone who is smartly dressed than to someone with a more casual look.

| Presentation | Suggested Dress code |
|---|---|
| College presentation | Casual OK, but not too casual |
| Job application | Smart, perhaps formal or casual |
| New idea or development | Slightly more smart than usual |
| School board | Formal probably preferred |
| Zoning board | Formal probably preferred |
| Sales pitch | Smart but comfortable |

The way you dress is an important part of the first impression you create. As a rule of thumb, you should be at least as formal as your audience, preferably a little more so. You can turn up in a dinner suit to address a crowd who are dressed casually, but the reverse doesn't work at all. It's often said that when you are badly dressed, people notice the dress, and when you are well dressed, people notice the person.

Whatever you wear, make sure you are comfortable. You need to be comfortable enough to concentrate on your delivery without the distraction of shoes that hurt, a waistband or collar that's too tight, or clothing that keeps you too warm or too cold.

Clothing can be particularly important if you are going to wear a lapel mike. When nylon shirts were more fashionable than now, I attended a presentation where the presenter wore a jacket over a nylon shirt. The problem was static electricity — the shirt crackled so much that we could hardly hear what was said.

Gender. Men may look at you and notice how you are dressed, but women seem more likely to observe a tie that doesn't match a shirt, socks that don't match anything, or unpolished shoes.

If possible, try to wear a color that contrasts with your background. A dark shirt is hardly conspicuous against a dark background.

**VISIBILITY HORROR STORY**

The large audience sat in rows, eager to be briefed by a major retail company. Two screens were available so that all had a good view of at least one of them. Between the screens was a platform for the speakers, with a lectern to one side. Most of the day's speakers traveled back and forth across the platform as they spoke. Those of the audience who looked down at their notes looked up and struggled to place the speaker against a cluttered background of doors, emergency exit signs and other distractions. A backdrop in a muted color would have helped enormously.

PRESENTATION PURPOSE
– inform and motivate audience about retail opportunities

PROBLEMS
– poor use of venue
– presenters' clothing didn't stand out against background

RESULT
– audience not optimally informed or motivated

SOLUTIONS
– check the venue
– check sight lines, audience viewpoints, background colors

## 3.4 USING LANGUAGE

**Your voice is the vehicle for this essential tool**

It seems so obvious, but language is another vital tool. In any presentation, you have to choose words to convey information, and that choice should be informed by the character of your audience and the purpose and nature of the presentation. An audience of professionals will expect relevant vocabulary, whereas an audience of the general public will probably benefit from a minimum of jargon.

For a local audience, where there is a strong local dialect, it's useful to work in a reference, in that dialect, to some topical event. President Kennedy's famous "Ich bin ein Berliner" may have been grammatically poor, but was effective in winning over his audience.

Slang is particularly difficult for several reasons. First, it is ever changing, and out-of-date slang simply sends the message that you have not kept up with it. Slang can also be very parochial, and the slang you understand and use may be unknown in another community. As a form of shorthand, slang works in the context and community in which it arises, but may be counterproductive elsewhere. 'Welcome all y'all' would work in the southern USA, but not so much in New

York or Washington. It's a judgment you have to make, and your audience research should help you to decide.

A conference presentation, with an audience drawn from a wider area, perhaps even international, will benefit from straightforward language.

Try to keep your language simple, with fairly short sentences and conversational vocabulary. Here are two contrasting examples.

*"Ladies and gentlemen, my topic for this presentation is one which I anticipate will further your financial aspirations and enhance your entrepreneurial expectations."*

*"Ladies and gentlemen, this morning I'm going to try to show you how to make more money."*

Which example makes the point more clearly?

### Vocabulary

A key tool in any communicator's toolbox is vocabulary. The key question is: Do you have the right vocabulary for your intended audience? Perhaps your audience will be specialists of some kind, in which case you have to make sure that you understand at least the basics of their vocabulary so that you use it correctly.

Less obvious might be the common use of certain words, as against their stricter meaning. These days, the word impact is very common. For many, an impact is a dramatic collision, and the word is misapplied more often than not. A different audience might be able to discern the difference between 'effect' as a verb and as a noun.

"To effect change is difficult," meaning that it isn't easy to make change happen.

"The effect of change is unpredictable," meaning that one cannot always tell what will happen during a period of change.

"His decision affected the change of plan," meaning that what he decided influenced the plan.

In the last two examples, the word impact might be acceptable to a more general audience.

Awesome is a word that has been so overused as to be valueless. To say that an audience question or suggestion is awesome is to say little other than that it is probably positive. Is your audience likely to accept awesome in that context as positive, or might they better appreciate reactions such as interesting, subtle, workable, or practicable?

Getgo is often used in place of start, but getgo line has yet to replace start line.

Selecting the right vocabulary isn't always easy. Pitch it too high and you can't get your message across. Pitch it too low and your audience is likely to feel irritated. Either way, you reduce your chances of achieving your purpose.

Back in 2002, I delivered two presentations dealing with a century of radio. The first was to radio hams, who were happy to lap up tech talk about AM and FM, the ionosphere and "skip." The second was to a more general audience, and the emphasis switched to radio occasions such as the Titanic, the first commercial radio broadcasts, "War of the Worlds," etc.

We're not just talking about set piece presentations to an organized audience. Twice in recent years, I had to deal with financial advisors who were fluent in their own financial vocabulary, but failed utterly to put their case to me in simple language that I could understand. In both cases the purpose of their presentation was to retain my business. In both cases they failed, not because they were incompetent at their job, but because they lacked basic presentation skills. They are among the reasons why this book has been written.

### Ethnicity

Ethnicity can be a presentation nightmare. Do you know the ethnic mix of your audience? Will their ethnicity make a difference to what you have to say or how you might say it? Certainly it might. Tread carefully into the waters of trying to appeal to an ethnicity other than your own. You have two options. Learn and understand the various ethnicities of your audience so thoroughly that you can use their vocabulary with ease, and safely negotiate any sensitivities. The other option is to stick firmly to your purpose, and to the language related to that purpose. That has been my approach, and for me it has worked. It was once suggested by an audience member that I was ignoring the ethnic (largely Latino) element of my audience. I agreed, and pointed out that since my purpose was independent of ethnicity, I had not addressed it. My questioner understood and accepted that, and I learned to make a point of stating my purpose clearly, and sticking to it. If it comes up, I invite guidance from the audience, and that works too.

### 3.5 Timing

**You can't always choose the date or time of your presentation, but if you can…**

A presentation to a colleague (remember that a presentation is about purpose, not about the size of the audience) might have to be made at a moment's notice and perhaps at the end of the day. An invitation to speak to a group may be at a time to suit the event or the program rather than you or your purpose.

Given any choice in the matter, it's usually best to speak early in the day. Not everyone is at their best first thing, and you might be among that number, but later in the day people have had more to think about, and later still they're already thinking about tomorrow.

Should you need to catch a colleague, you probably already know their style and whether they need a little time to get into the working day, or whether it's best to catch them as they hang up their coat. Or it might be that they are most receptive at some specific point in the day. You'll also know the worst times for them, and be keen to avoid those. Whatever you plan, it might be that you just have to do it at a time that really isn't good for either of you, and that's when your presentation skills will be most useful and most necessary.

Working with a group presents similar challenges. Whatever the time, some people will be at their best, and some will not, and your presentation skills will be the key to achieving your purpose.

A Rotary Club might meet for breakfast, lunch, or dinner. A breakfast or lunch club will expect you to stick closely to the allocated time (usually 20 to 30 minutes) while a dinner club may be more relaxed about timing. Whatever your audience, they will have time expectations, and a good presenter will adjust to that. In a conference setting, you may find that earlier speakers or workshops run over, and you suddenly find yourself asked to take less time (rarely does the reverse occur). Good planning and effective rehearsal will help you work to the allotted time, and prune if necessary.

The start of any presentation is an important step. Start speaking while the audience members are settling, and they are likely to miss your opening words. Wait too long to start speaking, and the audience can become restless. There is no formula to tell you the precise moment to start. You will learn with experience, and even then, you won't always get it right. With practice and perseverance, you will get it right more often. As mentioned earlier, having a question, challenge or judgment as your title will help to get you started.

Don't be afraid to stop speaking and let your audience have a good look at an image. Pause to let a point sink in, or to give their imagination time to really work on the scene you've just described or the story you've just told. Don't make the pause too long. Experience will help you to judge how long it should be, but as a rough guide, the noise level is low as people think, and slowly rises as more and more people "get it." Let it rise a little before moving on.

At the planning stage, estimate two slides per minute, and adjust according to what you need to say for each slide, the complexity or simplicity of the information per slide, etc.

**❹**

# Preparing

*Prepare – the plan you have drawn up, and the steps necessary to enact it.*

## 4.1 PHYSICAL ASPECTS

How tall are you? Could your height be a problem if you have to stand behind a lectern or work with a flip chart? Could your girth be a problem if you have to thread your way between others to get into position? Do whatever you have to do to make things easy for yourself. Ask for a small platform to stand on if the lectern is too high for you. Ask for something to raise the lectern if it's too low for you. Walk to the front of a stage if you feel you need to be seen more clearly. Standing tall also helps you to appear confident, and to project your voice better.

Do you have physical mannerisms? I have a friend who always scratches his chin before speaking, and I am not alone in my tendency to wave my hands around when talking. Women with long hair often sweep it back quite frequently, and if they are wearing wrist jewelry that jangles, that adds to the distraction. People may be chin strokers, ear tuggers, hand wringers, wrist flexers, or spectacle adjusters. Some people can stand in one position on a stage and deliver an entire presentation from that spot. Others feel more comfortable prowling around. Awareness doesn't mean eliminating such things, but they can provide a major distraction for the audience if not limited.

### Miscellaneous

Here are some mistakes you only ever make once. I've done or seen all of these.

- Forget to visit the bathroom beforehand and have to battle with your bladder pressure toward the end of the presentation.
- Eat curry beforehand, and watch the rest of the platform party wince as you breathe toward them.
- Forget to check trouser flies, shirt or blouse buttons before taking center stage.
- Eat beans beforehand, and have at least 50% of your attention on attempting to pass gas unobtrusively.
- Eat something you enjoy, but you know it gives you indigestion, and have the rumblings of your stomach broadcast over the PA.
- Pick up the wrong glasses, and stand there with your driving pair instead of your reading pair.
- Wear mismatching socks or shoes.
- At the meal preceding your presentation, spill sauce on your shirt or tie, and not have a spare anywhere to hand.
- At the meal preceding your presentation, spill sauce on your shirt or tie and don't notice it.

### Food and Drink

Many a presenter has done all the preparation only to fall at the last hurdle. I've watched an experienced professional stand up and find himself able to utter no more than a squeak. He had gulped down a glass of chilled milk a few minutes beforehand, and that was a mistake. The milk dried his mouth, and the chill had constricted his throat. It does that to some people. He was out of action for a good five minutes. I have learned that cold drinks of any kind have an adverse effect on my voice, so I avoid those before presenting.

Tempting though it may be, it is also sound advice to avoid tea and coffee beforehand. They too will tend to dry the throat, the caffeine can amplify any nervous tension you may have, and Murphy's Law suggests that the diuretic effect of coffee will always come into play during rather than after your presentation. I stick to decaf, but even so…

Many speakers consider the ideal drink to be room temperature water with a dash of lemon. The water is gentle on your throat and lemon helps reduce the build-up of mucus in the throat, so you shouldn't have to clear it so often. When you find a recipe that works for you, stick to it. Make it a habit to have a glass of water handy during your presentation. You may not always use it, but it'll be there when you need it.

Another temptation to avoid is alcohol or other drugs to relax yourself beforehand. Drugs may relax you, but there's a price. You won't be as sharp and it will show. It doesn't happen often, but if you've ever had to endure a presentation by someone who has been drinking or taking drugs — you'll know it makes no sense.

**VENUE HORROR STORY**

It is a bright sunny day, but a biting wind makes it preferable to be inside looking out at it. An audience assembles to hear a leading politician make a keynote speech. Coffee is served in a bright airy room with views out over the neighboring golf course. The presentation room, by contrast, is gloomy and crowded, with poor sight lines and inadequate ventilation. Whatever anticipation has been fostered by the anteroom is quickly dispelled in the oppressive atmosphere. Fortunately the politician has good news to convey, so that interest levels are lifted, but later in the day a more conventional presentation struggles.

PRESENTATION PURPOSE
– to inform audience

THE PROBLEM
– poor venue selection

RESULT
– audience less than optimally informed

SOLUTIONS
– check the venue
– use audience engagement techniques

**Where?**

Sometimes you are asked to do a presentation on short notice. Perhaps a board meeting in ten minutes, or a team meeting in a spare room. On short notice, you may not have much control over the place, or much of a chance to check it out. Given more notice, you should find out what you can.

For larger audiences, such as at a conference, this is probably the biggest variable faced by a presenter, and it pays to research the venue as thoroughly as possible. You may not be able to control the seating arrangements, etc., but you should find out what to expect. Many a good presentation has been marred by such elementary precautions as failing to disconnect that phone on the table in the corner.

Where is the presentation to be delivered? Make sure you have the address right, and these days a quick check on Google Maps or an app such as "Streets" will help get you there and suggest parking options. You may already know the room, and if you don't, try to find out what you can. For example if it's in a hotel, call the hotel, and ask if you can see a similar room. Conference and meeting venues are enormously varied, so inspect or research each one. Whenever possible, give yourself plenty of time to check things out well in advance so that you know where everything is. And be aware that what the venue says it has, may not always turn out to be what it actually has.

**What to look for in the venue...**

WIFI

These days it's almost automatic to check local WiFi, but for your presentation, go one step further and check the speed. I was once almost caught out by this. I had created a presentation using Google Slides and planned to deliver it on-line. On arrival I checked wifi access, and was able to see the file. About 15 minutes before I was due to go on, I decided to make a last-minute change and found that the connection speed was too slow. Fortunately I had a spare copy on a flash drive in a corner of my bag, and that saved the day. Ever since, I check not just the access, but the speed, even if I'm not using Google Slides. Even if you don't have the entire presentation online, you might plan to go on-line at some point to connect to a live website or other resource. This will always be risky. In any setting, how many others are using wifi and slowing it down? Better by far to have everything you are likely to need on your laptop, backed up on a flash drive.

Some years ago, when WiFi was still relatively new, I had to do a presentation to parents at a school. I arrived early to work with the custodian and have everything ready for the evening meeting. The WiFi signal was strong, which was important because the presentation included one link to a website. When the time came and I clicked on the link, there was nothing. Fortunately I had a screen shot of the home page available and was able to bring that up within a few seconds. The problem was simple. The WiFi router was in the school office, and when that closed for the day, everything was switched off. Another lesson learned.

Speedtest.net is a popular speed test, but there are several others to choose from. The speed you need depends on the complexity of your presentation, but as a general rule, you should be looking for a speed comparable to the speed at home or in your office — wherever you develop and rehearse the presentation. But don't ever depend on it — always have that backup.

YOUR POSITION

Create the working space you need for your presentation. Make sure it is big enough, and has the facilities you need to succeed in achieving your purpose.

Are you in plain view or will you be out of sight and brought on after an introduction?

Do you have to walk to where you will be presenting, and if so, are there any obstacles to stumble over or avoid? Examples might be microphone or power cables, briefcases or other bags, changes in platform level, joints in platform modules, chair legs, etc.

Where will you be standing (and you should stand)? Sitting compresses you. Standing up will allow you to breathe better, and speak better. Sitting or standing, make sure you can reach all the resources you plan to use. Check the chair you plan to use, to make sure it doesn't creak or squeak, and is safe.

Will you have a lectern or table to stand behind, which means you have somewhere to put notes and other props, but are partially hidden from view? A lectern or a table also gives you something to lean on, whether from behind or to the side, and to place notes or props on.

Will you be out in the open, in full view but with nowhere to place notes? Whichever it is, make sure you have a clock visible. Your laptop or table has the time on the screen, but that may not be easy enough to see from a distance. Any smartphone will do. Position it so that you can see it easily, especially if you're going to move about.

### Lectern Pros and Cons

| PRO | CON |
|---|---|
| Gives you something to hold | May limit your use of gestures |
| Fixes your position | Inhibits your movement |
| Place to put notes | May inhibit eye contact with audience |
| Place to put props | Can get cluttered |
| May have mike attached, which looks neat | Mike may pick up paper rustling and other noises |
| May include controls to allow you to adjust lighting, etc. | You have to learn which switch does what |
| May be adjustable in height | Getting it adjusted |

*TABLE 3*

### Table Pros and Cons

| PRO | CON |
|---|---|
| Provides place for notes | May be too low to see notes clearly |
| Provides place for props | Audience sees props beforehand |
| Allows movement away if necessary | May encourage too much movement |
| Allows use of table stand for mike | Table stand can pick up extraneous noise |

*TABLE 4*

It's all a matter of personal choice, but a really versatile position is slightly to the left side, with a table to your offstage side (right if you're right-handed). Add a lectern on the end of the table nearest you. If sound reinforcement is needed, position a mike stand in front of the lectern with the mike (preferably on a gooseneck or short boom arm) coming over the top of the lectern.

**This arrangement**
- places your notes at a convenient height for easy reference
- provides space for laser pointer and other props
- allows you to move center stage when you wish to
- enables you to make full use of gestures
- works with a screen in the center or to your side

If you are working with a flip chart, take a more central position, with the flip chart to one side (left side if you are right-handed) and the table to the other. Two flip charts are even better, since one can be used for main points, and the other for detail or for audience responses, questions, etc.

LIGHTING

Is the lighting comfortable and consistent for the audience, and controllable for you? Some venues may have lights that highlight you, but may make it difficult for you to see your audience, and may also make it difficult for people to see a screen. Others may have lights that are controlled from wall switches at the rear of the room, so that you need an assistant to make any necessary adjustments. Conference and hotel venues will usually be able to light you without dazzling you. Depending on your purpose, you may want medium or full Front of House (FOH) lighting so that you can see your audience. Have someone take care of that for you so that you can stay focused on your delivery.

Does the room have windows, and what is the effect of the daylighting? You might need to draw curtains or lower blinds, and it helps to know where the sunshine will be at the time of your presentation. More than one presentation has been marred by a slice of sunlight seeping past the edge of an ill-fitting blind and falling on the projection screen where it obliterates that carefully prepared image. Make sure that same slice of sunlight doesn't affect some of your audience.

Have someone take care of lighting and curtains for you so that you can stay focused on your delivery.

TEMPERATURE

Is the room warm enough (or cold enough) to be comfortable? Either extreme is likely to have your audience focused on their comfort rather than your presentation, and so will threaten your ability to achieve your purpose. Too warm and they'll all be dozing off.

## SOUNDS

Listen to the room. Do you hear the noise of heating or air conditioning, of a nearby elevator or kitchen, an adjacent restroom or public corridor, etc.? If you're visiting the room the evening before, what daytime noises are you missing? Look around to see if there is a construction site next door; and in a hotel or multi-use conference center, it helps to check with the management to see what else is going on. A noisy conference next door might oblige you to use sound reinforcement that otherwise you might not need.

Speaking at a conference in the meeting rooms of a sports stadium, I was interrupted by an outburst of song from the kitchen next door. Apparently, the organizers had forgotten to inform the chef, whose habit was to entertain the kitchen as he undertook preparations. Someone dashed next door to explain the situation and we were able to proceed.

Often you can check on the reverberation of the room by clapping your hands. Reverberation is the echo that you get from bare walls and ceilings. A modest amount of reverberation is helpful, and the handclap allows you to hear how the sound echoes and dies away. People soak up sound, reduce the echo, and reduce the reverberation, so an empty room usually sounds "brighter" than a full one.

Too much reverberation isn't helpful. Speak too quickly, and one word is still bouncing around as the next one arrives, and the audience will have difficulty. You have to slow down your pace so that each word has time to die away before the next one arrives. Obviously, a short presentation will be less affected. A longer one may need some pruning to avoid running over. A room with no echo (anechoic) is fine, but you probably need to speak up a bit.

## SEATING

You may have no control over this, for example when invited to present at a conference, but seating arrangements can help or hinder your efforts to achieve your purpose. Obvious examples would include not enough seats for the audience size, far too many for the audience size, uncomfortable seats, etc. It is sometimes better to lay out too few chairs and be ready to set out more as people arrive. This suggests a popular presentation and great demand. Having only half the chairs occupied suggests a less popular presentation. If you have your target audience, this may not matter much, but if you are trying to build a reputation as a presenter, it could make a difference.

One thing you'll notice is that quite often, the front row remains empty, or is occupied last. If faced with an empty front row, I usually remark on how pointless it is to set out a front row, since nobody ever sits there.

There are a handful of classic seating arrangements, and you may or may not be able to influence that, if you want to.

## 1. Classroom

Rows of seats, with people placed close together is one of the most frequently used for several reasons. It's easier for the staff to set out and retrieve the chairs. Seat positions can be identified and allocated, if need be, and it's efficient in packing a large number of people into a small space. From your point of view, there are four sets of people you need to worry about in this arrangement.

First, the center front. Anyone who sits in the front row is usually there for a reason. Maybe they were too late to get a seat farther back and had to take the least popular places. Maybe they wanted to be there. If you're lucky, that's because they were very interested in you or your topic, but it could be that they want to be in prime position to catch your eye and get their questions answered. Either way, they and you are hostages to each other. They can hardly escape your attention, and you can hardly escape theirs. For the front row, height may also be a problem. If they are too close, a presenter or screen that is high enough to be visible from the back may be awkward to see from the front.

Next, the back row. If they chose the back row, they probably are more interested in getting out fast at the end than in listening to you. They are also the ones who have to look across or between more heads than anyone else, so you have to make sure that you and any aids you use are high enough to be fully visible to them.

Third, the people at the left and right ends of the front row. It's more often than not the case that the rows are pushed well forward to maximize the audience, but those at the front corners have to turn to see you and are worst placed to see a projection screen if it's on the wall behind you — a favorite place for it. They are prisoners of their position, and you need to free them so that they can see, either by inviting them to move, or by arranging your presentation so that it is visible to them. A corner screen will often be the answer. They may still need to turn a little, but at least they will see.

Fourth, check for pillars in the room, and those who may be placed with a restricted view. It's easier to keep their attention if they can see clearly. If the seating is movable, try to remove any seats that are directly behind pillars. People are unlikely to sit there unless the place is packed, but if they are, make a point of moving to the side from time to time so that they can see you, and look directly at them so that they know you haven't forgotten them and aren't ignoring them.

### 2. Table Seating

Groups at a table are a common conference format, and a useful one. People have a place for books and notes, can get to know each other, and undertake group tasks. For a presentation, you have to face the problem that some of your audience has to shuffle around to be able to see you, and it's a good idea to give them a few seconds to do that before you start. Don't just wait and expect it to happen. Encourage them, even suggest that it will be worth the effort. As with the classroom layout, there may be hostages in the front group, or prisoners hidden behind large table decorations or at the corner tables.

### 3.  U layout

Small meetings are often arranged with people round three sides of a rectangle formed by tables. Sometimes the rectangle is closed by the tables, but the longer the rectangle, the more difficult it is for those in the far corners to see. A better arrangement is to open them out so that there is a space in the middle. This makes it easier for everybody to see each other, which is why it is popular for workshops and interactive meetings. The open U also allows a presenter to wander down among the audience. Think carefully about this. The advantage is that it brings you into closer contact, which might be useful, but can also be seen as a little intimidating. The main problem is that as you advance and turn to the left or right, you turn your back to the other side, and how do you return without turning your back on everyone?

### 4.  The Auditorium

An auditorium may have tiered seats on a raked floor, or they may be all on the same level. There may be one or more access aisles, and even one or more cross aisles. A theater-style auditorium may have the audience in a long narrow zone stretching away from you. Others may have a semi-circular arrangement, with people well out to each side of you. It pays to try out the seats, especially those in the far and near corners, and any balcony areas, so that you understand the audience view of the stage. Whatever the arrangement, you need to make sure that you make eye contact with all areas from time to time. It's all too easy in a large venue to concentrate on those directly in front of you, and you may need to write reminders into your notes so that you look to the extreme left and right, or to the balcony.

The impersonality of an auditorium is a barrier. The lighting may make it difficult to see people, but if you can get on the stage beforehand, you can check sight lines so that you know in which direction to look to see people. I was once well into a presentation before my eyes adjusted sufficiently to the spotlights to let me see that one area to which I had been nodding and smiling was almost empty of people.

On a stage, you may be faced with a set layout. Sometimes those setting out a stage do so with convenience or aesthetics in mind. The tables and chairs may be set where it is easiest to put them, or from where it is easiest to remove them, or even where it is easiest to light them. Whatever the rationale behind the layout, you need to assess whether it works for you, and try to change it if it doesn't. You may need to assert that it's your presentation and purpose, and not be intimidated by any barriers placed in your path.

**You need to**
- be well to the front of the stage, so that all can see and hear you
- be able to see the audience without being dazzled by the lighting
- have the space you are comfortable with
- have the space you need for any aids you use
- have space in which to move if you need to
- ensure good visibility of any screens or other aids you use
- have control of house lighting if it needs to be lowered (either directly or by means of an agreed cue to an assistant)
- ensure a comfortable temperature so that both you and your audience can focus on your purpose

Whatever the layout, your task is to make sure it works for you and for your audience. Prior research is essential to making sure that happens.

**VENUE HORROR STORY**

The audience assembled in a small theater with plush seating and expansive areas of heavy velvet curtains. Hosting was a by a technology organization, so expectations were high. The presentation began, and the first speaker used a microphone. Since the décor absorbed sound, there was sufficient audio output for him to be heard, but only just. It appeared that the audio system was cranked up to maximum power, and it wasn't enough. The second speaker failed to adjust the microphone height, and was inaudible beyond the first few rows. Those at the rear could see mouth movements, but heard nothing.

PRESENTATION PURPOSE
– to engage and inform audience

PROBLEMS
– inadequate audio power for the room

RESULT
– audience disengaged and less informed

SOLUTIONS
– practice with equipment
– discover and rectify power problem

## 4.3 CONSIDERING ROOM LAYOUT

On short notice, you may have to perform "on the spot." If time allows, you may be able to influence the seating arrangement of the venue in order to help you achieve that purpose.

Focus on your working area. You need to be in a position where you and your visual aids are clearly visible. There are a few options to consider.

First, a table. This is good since it usually gives you room for things such as a laptop and projector, plus any notes you may have. My preference is to stand at the left side of the table, with my laptop near me so I can see the screen. The projector sits beside it pointing to a screen behind me to my right (or is ceiling mounted). Once the projector is set and focused, all I need to see is the laptop screen, so I can stay facing the audience.

The table also has room for any props or other resources I need. Sometimes the table is smaller, perhaps card table size, with space for only the projector, in which case I've used a chair with a box on it, or even a stack of chairs. If the laptop is low on a chair, the remote control comes into its own, allowing me to change slides without having to bend down to the laptop. And at times like these, a tablet on a mike stand can also save the day (if you have the right connectors).

Second, a lectern. Conference areas, universities and libraries may have a floor-standing lectern with all the switches you need built in. There is room for the laptop, and the HDMI cable to a ceiling mounted projector is there. Also, you have control of the light switches, and a mike stand and mike are included. We'll come back to that mike later.

Another lectern may have a flat surface, often with higher edges so that your laptop and other resources are concealed, or it may have a sloping surface. The flat surface is useful if it has space for your laptop and/or notes, and the screen is low enough that you can see and be seen over it. A lectern with a sloping surface is built for speakers such as politicians and lecturers who can place their notes on the slope where they can refer to them (or perhaps even just read them). For presenters, a sloping lectern, may make it difficult to position the laptop since you may be partly concealed behind it. You don't want the laptop or tablet sliding off, and a short strip of gaffa tape will enable you to hold it in place.

The lectern-mounted mike can be a problem. I always carry a shockmount for microphones. Any lectern mike is prone to picking up all the noises made on the lectern. Any time you knock against it, shuffle the pages of your notes, or move a resource, the mike is likely to pick that up. A shockmount, or a mike on a floor stand beside the lectern, is the cure. A shockmount is a mike holder that has a rubber element that isolates the mike from noise coming up through the stand — or in this case, the lectern. If you use your own mike, make sure you get a shock-mount to go with it.

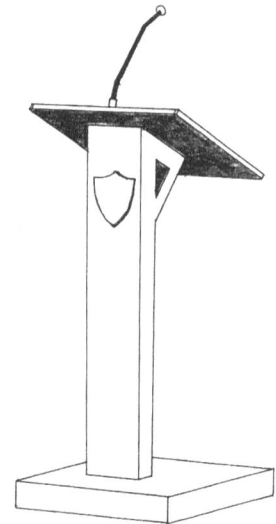

*Figure 13. Lectern*

Beware the lectern with the built-in loudspeaker. Some venues will provide a lectern with an amplifier on a lower shelf, and a speaker or speakers projecting sound from the front. These are usually designed to be used on a stage, in which case the sound will be projected toward the seated audience at approximately head height. In that context, it works fine. That same lectern, used at floor level, projects the sound into the front row of the audience, and those at the back may have difficulty hearing.

Sometimes there will be a smaller lectern that sits on a table. That takes up room on the table which you might otherwise want to use, and it is more likely to have a sloping surface. If there is no lectern, just use a table. If you need the laptop to be a little higher and more visible, use a box, and drape a cloth over it.

### Screen Position (if you have a choice)

There's always a temptation to have a screen front and center, cinema style. That's where you'll usually find fixed screens in hotels, libraries and conference centers.

In this layout, the presenter is forced to the corners, but it provides excellent visibility if the screen is high enough and/or the audience is in raked seats (as in most movie theaters). It's useful if the majority of the presentation is screen based.

*Figure 14. Central Screen*

In a normal room, visibility can be improved by staggering the seating, so that one row looks between the people in the row in front of them.

A good alternative is to move the screen to a corner, which enables the presenter to be center stage.

*Figure 15. Screen in corner*

*Figure 16. Conventional classroom*

Switching audience attention between screen and presenter involves a little movement, which helps keep their general attention, but the presenter must allow for that movement and the associated temporary distraction.

This is a regimented layout and very common, especially in long narrow rooms. Janitorial/custodial staff love it because it looks neat and tidy. Cleaners love it because it's easy to get along between the rows with brooms or vacuum cleaners.

Presenters usually groan a little when they see this one. The straight rows may look neat, but the sight lines aren't always too good, although the presenter has everyone within a narrow field of view which makes it easier to maintain eye contact with everyone. Those at the back may find it difficult to see clearly, and so lose a little interest. If some of the audience can't see you too well, try to move around a little during your presentation to compensate.

A narrow room gives you less space in which to set out flip charts or a screen, or any other aids or props that you may need.

It's OK for flip charts since they can be high enough to be visible, but if you need to place a projector it can be awkward. If it's a wide-angle projector you can use that center desk in the front row, but a narrow angle projector will need to be further back, in among your audience.

There may be a ceiling-mounted projector, which usually implies a central screen on the wall behind you, and a place to plug in your HDMI cable from your laptop. A longer HDMI cable will give you more flexibility in your choice of position.

*Figure 17. Angled Rows*
Angling the rows slightly gives a big general improvement in
sight lines and helps the audience to feel more involved.

*Figure 18. Workshop Layout*
Should you need your audience to spend most of their time working in small groups, this
arrangement works well. People sit around the tables to work with each other, but some
have to turn around to see you, so this works only if your input is brief and occasional.

*Figure 19. U Layout*

This is a popular and useful setup for small groups, especially if interchange between participants is important. Sight lines are fair, and can be improved if the left and right sides are angled even slightly. Presenters have plenty of space for aids, devices and props, and a projector can be placed and accessed in the center.

*Figure 20. V Layout*

This offers similar pros and cons to the U-shaped layout, but works well only with small numbers. In this case, a flip chart is centrally placed.

*Figure 21. Lecture Theater Layout*

The seats are arranged here with the presenter's position as the focal point. If that is what is needed, this is a good layout, and understandably popular for lectures involving a minimum of visual aids. The greater the distance between the presenter and the curve, the better the audience view, and the more space the presenter has for aids and devices. Sight lines are generally good, and although some audience interaction is possible, it isn't ideal.

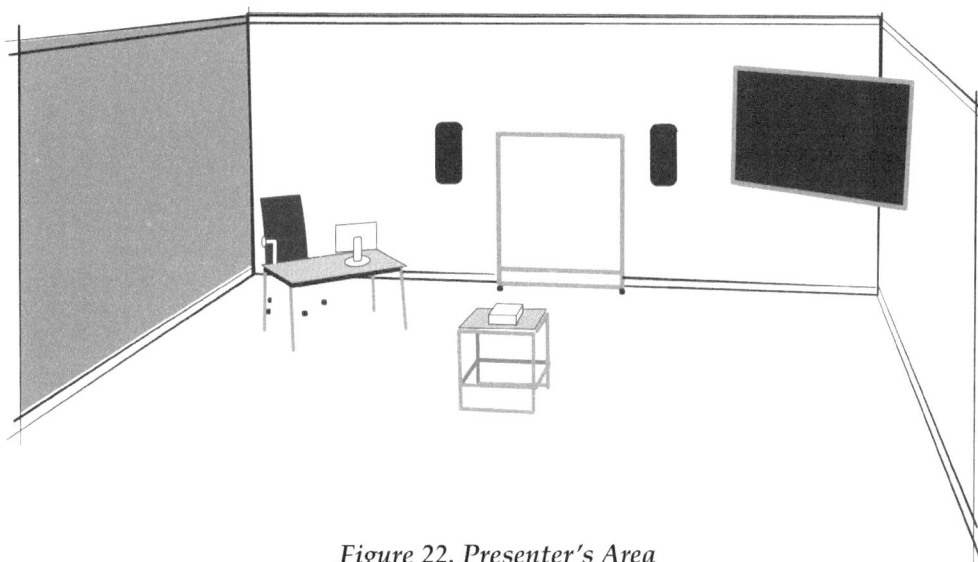

*Figure 22. Presenter's Area*

In a formal presentation, it's important to be comfortable. That means having space to lay out what you need, a position for your laptop that makes it easily visible, short distances between essential equipment, and no cables to trip over. In this layout, the presenter can move fairly easily between the various devices, and has a table for notes, props, etc.

Flip chart pens can be stored on the table and on the easel.

A right-handed presenter can stay to the side of the projector, but central to the room, and easily stay out of the line of sight of the audience

The power cable for the data projector should come from the near side of the room. Have enough cable to connect the laptop on the table to the data projector.

### Variations

Some data projector stands have space for the laptop too. Using a remote control unit frees the presenter once the presentation begins.

Place the PA or speaker below or beside the screen, especially if video with sound is part of the presentation.

*Figure 23. Fixed screen*

This is the classic fixed screen position, so the flip chart is to the side. It provides excellent visibility for the audience if the screen is high enough and/or the audience is in raked seats (e.g. in many movie theaters). It's useful if the majority of the presentation is screen based.

In a normal room, visibility can be improved by staggering the seating, so that one row looks between the people in the row in front of them.

With a central screen, the presenter is forced to the corners, and the left side, as seen by the audience, is best. If the screen is fixed, other resources such as a lectern may also be fixed, and not necessarily in the best place.

With a PowerPoint or Keynote presentation, one option is to use the B key to blank the screen, drawing attention back to the presenter.

*Figure 24. Screen to side*

### Screen to One Side and Angled

A good alternative is to move the screen to a corner, which enables the presenter to be center stage or slightly left of center. as seen by the audience. A table can be placed farther left for props, notes, a laptop, etc. Here, the flip chart is in the middle.

The presenter is able to take a more central position, and is likely to have a little more space to move around.

### Cord and Cable Runs

One problem that nearly always arises is the power cords for equipment. The worst thing to do is to have power cords, HDMI cables, mike cables, etc., loose on the floor in various places. Wherever possible these should be in areas of little or no foot traffic, straight, and taped down with gaffa tape, or concealed in cord covers. If nothing else is available, use duct tape, but carefully. Gaffa tape will peel off leaving no residue. Duct tape might take some paint with it.

Perhaps you'll be presenting in a space where all this is taken care of for you. When presenting in a place that I haven't been able to scout, I've learned to have a reel of power cord, a spare distribution strip, and spares of all the USB and audio cables I might need. Experience also teaches that what the venue says it has, may not always turn out to be what it actually has. Caveat presenter!

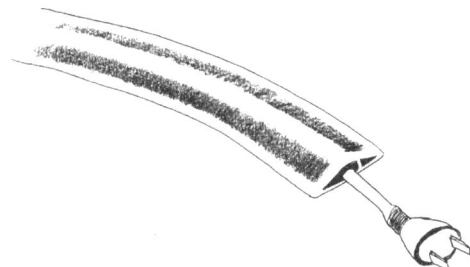

*Figure 25. Power cord in cover*

## 4.4 WORKING WITH PROPS

**A carefully selected and well used prop can help you to make your point, and achieve your purpose.**

Sometimes a point can be made very effectively, even dramatically using a prop. A good prop can often be available at short notice, or even suggest itself during a presentation.

An effective example about law and order involved a police officer's hat on a hat stand to the right, and a burglar's stocking mask on a dummy head to the left. All the presenter had to do was move to one side or the other, or sometimes just look or gesture to the appropriate side. The simplest of props, and yet hugely cost effective.

In a workshop about public relations, the trainer used a glove puppet to demonstrate a point about communications. The naked hand said little, but clothed in the puppet, the same movements conveyed a message.

To make a point about computers, a presenter held up an ordinary pencil. The pencil, he said, was well designed for its purpose, but without human control, it could achieve nothing. The computer also needed human input, partly in its design, partly in the software, and ultimately, from the user. In that sense, even the smartest computer was no smarter than a pencil.

Another presenter made his entire presentation with a large object on the table beside him covered by a black cloth. Naturally enough the object drew attention. People wondered what was under it, and as the presentation progressed with no reference to it, that curiosity grew. Other objects were brought into play, but no reference was made to the hidden object. The presenter reached his conclusion, thanked the audience for listening and said that there was one thing he really wanted them to remember. He then drew aside the cloth to reveal a giant version of his business card.

An assistant, perhaps even a volunteer from the audience, can sometimes serve as a prop. While you can safely poke fun at yourself or a member of your own team, you have to be careful not to put a volunteer into any embarrassing situation. Silent participation is generally safe, where they hold something, or perform a simple operation such as waving a flag on cue, handing you items as required, etc. Remember to provide some form of reward for any volunteers.

Choosing a prop needs as much care and attention as anything else in the presentation. The prop needs to be:

- ✓ big and bold enough to be clearly visible to everybody
- ✓ small enough to be manageable
- ✓ obvious enough to make your point, and
- ✓ simple enough to be understood

Props are like an actor waiting offstage for a cue, and so often need to be hidden until needed, but may then be left on a table if you need to refer back to them. If you're on a stage, make sure the prop is to the front of the table so that it's visible, or simply pick it up again when necessary. Like the actor, once it has fulfilled its role, it should be hidden from view so that it is not a distraction. If it isn't in use — it's underware.

## AV RESOURCES HORROR STORY

The young man had won a scholarship, and was there to tell an audience of contributors what he was doing with it. He spoke well, and early in his talk he mentioned that a snippet of video was to be used. The screen and projector were indeed ready by his side. Reaching the critical point, he produced the video cassette, reached over to switch things on, inserted the cassette, and spent the next couple of minutes fiddling about trying to get a picture. Aided by a couple of the audience, he eventually succeeded, but had long since lost the attention of his audience, and undermined the positive impression he had been creating until then.

PURPOSE
– to thank scholarship contributors and encourage continued participation

PROBLEMS
– poor use of AV resource

RESULT
– audience not as encouraged as they might have been

SOLUTIONS
– have equipment switched on before start
– have videocassette cued up to correct start point

## 4.5. CHOOSING PRESENTATION SOFTWARE

### Is there a choice?

There are two. The first is whether or not to use presentation software. PowerPoint and its competitors need not necessarily be the first choice. If it suits your purpose to keep it simple, or if there is a better option, use it (see 2.4).

If you do decide to use presentation software, there is a wide choice.

In fact you are most likely to use whichever is most available, and there is little that differentiates them. All are powerful and sophisticated and allow for a wide range of creative possibilities.

Keynote comes free with every Apple computer or iPad, and so it's an obvious choice for Apple users like myself. It offers slightly fewer submenu facilities (distractions) which helps me to stay focused on my purpose.

*Figure 26.*
*Software icons*

PowerPoint is part of the Microsoft Office package for PCs which makes it the obvious choice for MS Office users. Starting with either of these may well give you all that you need for the presentations you do and the purposes you need to achieve.

There are other options on both platforms, and while I don't intend to set out a comprehensive comparison, here are a few things to think about before going shopping for your regular presentation software.

### Simplicity

Both Keynote and PowerPoint offer impressive results with little effort. If all you need are captions and headings, a few images and some simple graphs or charts, both will provide that. Both offer a range of backgrounds and texts. Both offer animations so that your text or image can do more than just appear (slide in, drop in, burst into flames etc.), but be wary of overdoing these. Both allow you to decide the order in which text boxes and images appear on any slide, and both allow you to rearrange the sequence of your slides quickly and easily. Both come with an impressive library of images that can be used to enhance your presentation. Whichever you choose, stick to a consistent layout, preferably landscape.

### Cost

Keynote is a hands down winner for any Mac user since it comes free. Other free options include Google Slides and LibreOffice.

Google Slides is simple to use and has a range of effects, images, fonts etc., to satisfy most purposes. Access it from any computer, tablet or modern phone, and any work you do offline will update when you connect.

LibreOffice Impress has a more cluttered layout which can make it a little more difficult to negotiate, but once you get used to it, you have a comparable range of facilities, images, fonts, etc.

There are other free options to explore but a word of caution. Some offer a free introductory level, but charge for extra capabilities. It pays to start with the truly free options until your needs are clearer.

### Online or Offline

Do you want to work online, offline, or both?

PowerPoint, Keynote, LibreOffice and Google Slides all allow you to work offline and save your file. Google Slides files can be shared in Google Docs. The others can be shared in Dropbox or similar.

Personally I'm wary of relying completely on the online world. I once had a presentation to do in a library and had checked that it had free online access (most do). I had the presentation online, arrived early as usual, and set the laptop to work downloading my file. Closer to the start time I noticed that it hadn't finished. A hasty inquiry revealed that there was a limit on the download speed! Fortunately I had my iPad with me. It had the same file but I was intending to use the laptop as the source for the digital projector. Fortunately I had the appropriate connectors for the iPad and made them ready. The laptop download completed with one minute to spare. Since then I've never relied on the online world, but always make sure I have my presentation files saved on the iPad or laptop, or at least on a thumb drive.

### Online Cooperation

Some presentations will be solo efforts, so your choice of software is your decision. If collaboration is likely to be an important part of your presentation experience, you need more specialized software. Google Slides allows this at a simple level, but if you need to track exactly who did what, you'll need to step up to something more sophisticated.

### Your Style, Your Purpose

Do you like to start with a blank canvas, or use templates? PowerPoint and Keynote allow you to do either. Google Slides and LibreOffice start with templates, some of which might suit your purpose, but a clear canvas gives more flexibility. Whatever your style, stay with landscape format for your images. That means they fit both a projection screen, and a TV.

For some purposes, a basic style is all that is needed. You may not have enough time to do more than use simple captions for your main points. Or you may just prefer to keep it simple and straightforward, with minimum distractions for your audience. For other purposes, you may choose a more elaborate presentation style, with captions overlying a graphic background. It depends on your style, your preference, and your purpose.

My own preference is the simple basic style. As an audience member I find the elaborate styles distracting. As a presenter, I find it easier to keep things simple. I find it allows me more scope to develop and adjust a presentation. I can focus on the flow of the text without having to consider the flow of background graphics.

### What features do you need?

Most presentations involve three main elements — text, images, and video. Our four main contenders all handle these well. Text boxes, images and video are objects and can be superimposed on each other, hidden and revealed on a click or after a variable delay. All of these are the stuff of most presentations, and will satisfy many needs.

Video and music are where it gets interesting. Each of our four main contenders can handle audio and video, but in slightly different ways. Music and video files can usually be imported from the laptop (e.g., from iTunes or similar) or from an online source. Most formats can be handled (.wav, .aiff, .mp3, .mov, . mp4, etc.), but it's always worth checking to make sure that whichever software you plan to use is able to handle any audio or video format you plan to import.

The latest version of Keynote can now play an audio file over consecutive files. PowerPoint has been able to do this for some time.

Video can be imported in the same way and can be set to start automatically or after a delay. The start and finish of a video file can be trimmed so that you can select the part you want to include.

A bewildering range of animations allow you to select the way that objects arrive on the screen. They can appear, or dissolve in, which is usually a little less harsh. They can also fly, swirl, bounce, flip, etc. If such effects really serve your purpose, use them, but be aware that audiences tend to tire of these quite quickly. Similarly, slides can change by rotating, sliding in from any side, etc.

There is presentation software dedicated to sales and to church audiences, and software that allows sharing with the audience. Audience feedback can even be included if necessary.

Such specialized uses are beyond the scope of this book. The important point is that your choice of software depends on one basic consideration: Does it help you achieve your presentation purpose(s)?

**Presentation Software – Questions to Ask**
Is there a cost?
Is it one off, or subscription based?
Does it represent good value for me?
Is it flexible, or aimed at particular users (e.g., sales)?
Can slides be created?
Are templates available?
Is there an image library?
Is there a text editor?
Is it easy to use?
Is the presentation stored on a device, online, or both?
Can images be included (from file, or online)?
Can video be included (from file, or online)?
Can audio be included (from file, or online)?
Is there a presenter's view?
Is it multiplatform (laptop, tablet, phone etc.)?
Does it synchronize across platforms?
Is it versatile enough for my needs?
Is the result good enough for my purpose?

## 4.6 LAYERING AND ANIMATION

Layering and animation can be powerful visual aids. As with any of the range of effects, use them sparingly, and where they best serve your purpose.

When you add another text box, or a shape, perhaps as basic as a line, there are now two objects on the slide. They are the layers, and the default conditions are that they appear in the order in which they were created, and that the second and subsequent objects lie on top of the first. Think of them as pages lying on top of each other. They can be shuffled to appear in any order. The individual pages can be resized, and made more or less opaque. Animation means that they can appear in any number of ways including a simple appearance, a dissolve, etc.

The build order, or layering, is a very useful feature. This controls the order in which objects appear in a slide. They can appear 'on click', or after an adjustable delay. It may suit your purpose to have a slide built up in stages rather than have everything appear all at once.

This example is from an attempt to show the route of an old trolley line on the modern landscape. I found an old aerial photograph that showed the route, and added text to make it clearer. Since I do a number of these presentations in different areas, I can now do this very quickly, and audience feedback shows me that it is certainly a worthwhile effort.

A word of caution. Check the size of any image you intend to use. When magnified on a screen a low-resolution image will appear grainy. In some cases that might be acceptable — you have to be the judge.

*Figure 27. 1934 Landscape*

*Figure 28. Today's landscape*

Google Earth provided an image of today's landscape which I adjusted for size and laid on top of the first two.

I made the modern image semi opaque so that I could see the earlier landscape underneath and line them up. Restored to full opacity, I could set it for a slow dissolve. The old landscape appeared first, and on click, today's landscape, perfectly aligned, slowly replaced it. The technique gave the audience time to make sense of both images.

In a presentation about sustainability, I wanted to make a point, and decided to use an image of a sunset.

*Figure 29. Sunset 1*

*Figure 30. Sunset 2*

The background image appeared first, with the upper text following after a three second delay. I could have arranged to have the lower text appear on click, but decided to use a two second delay since that was a better match for what I had to say.

While rehearsing, I realized that the sunset would be much more impressive if the image took up the entire slide, and the final version is in Figure 30.

Images can extend beyond the slide area. The next image (Figure 31) is centered in the slide area, allowing space above and below for text. Because the image doesn't occupy the whole slide, I've used a black background.

Figure 31. Osprey 1

Figure 32. Osprey 2

The second image has been stretched to fill the entire slide area. Any text will have to be superimposed.

Next, the image stretches beyond the slide area. The support pole for the nest platform can be seen extended below, and the branches extend on the other three sides. Only that part of the image in the main slide area will appear on the screen when the presentation is played. The image has to be high resolution for this to work without appearing grainy.

Figure 33. Osprey 3

In this next example I wanted to make a point about the difference between ON and OFF. I could have used two successive slides, but using a single slide offered more options. First, the text and the OFF switch.

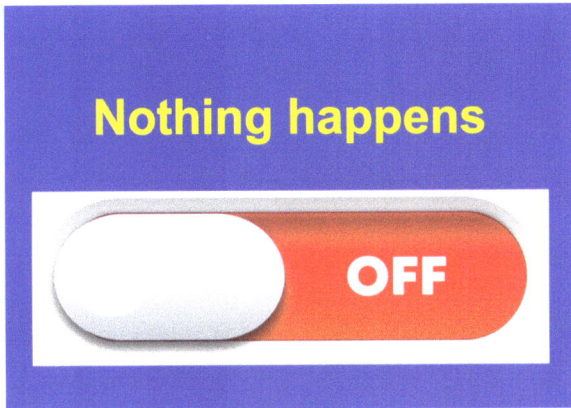

*Figure 34. Off*

*Figure 35. On*

I superimposed an ON switch of the same size, set to appear on click. At the same time, a blue rectangle covered up the word "Nothing," followed by the appearance of the word "Something," all carefully positioned. The result was that on click, both the switch and the text changed. The time and effort spent on this was worthwhile since I have been able to use it on several other occasions, sometimes to indicate the "switching on"of the presentation, or the start of a plan or campaign.

Images can be made semi-opaque. This faded effect is useful if you want to overlay text on an image. Start with the image, then add a white rectangle the same size as the image but 50% (or so) opaque. That gives the image a "washed out" appearance. Overlay text in a suitably contrasted color. Play with the settings to get the result you want.

This slide was about selecting the right tool for the job. I used an image of four different cameras.

*Figure 36. Cameras 1*

*Figure 37. Cameras 2*

Next, I added a white rectangle, and reduced its opacity so that the image appeared faded. Putting it off center, as shown, allowed me to judge the degree of opacity I wanted before sliding it into position. The text was added last, which meant it was on top.

The timing was that the camera image appeared first. The white image came next as a slow dissolve, so that the image appeared to fade, after which came the text.

*Figure 38. Cameras 3*

The same end result could be achieved by simply adjusting the opacity of the original image to give the washed-out appearance and then adding the text, but I felt it was more effective to show the clear image first, and then fade it before adding the text.

I sometimes use a variation on this technique for a title slide. To use it in a new presentation I drag it into the new presentation and change the two text layers. I use it often enough to make the effort worthwhile, and just as with an earlier technique, practice means I can now do it very quickly. It certainly works as an attention grabber at the start of a presentation.

A lamp appears, with a washed-out title. (Figure 39). On click, the lamp lights, and the title appears bright and bold.

*Figure 39. Lamp 1*

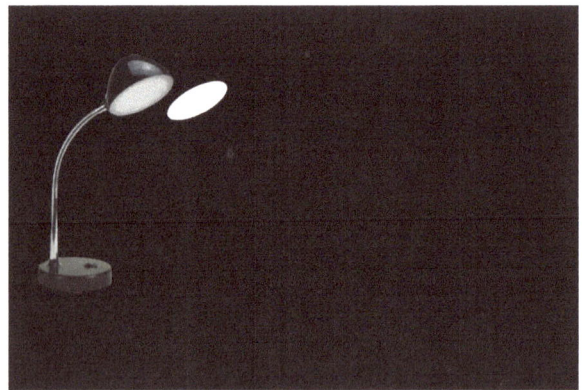

*Figure 40. Lamp 2*

**Preparing**

Here's the lamp, unlit, with the faded title to the right. To "light" the lamp, I superimpose a white oval — Figure 40. (A copy of that oval appears to the right of the lamp for illustration purposes.)

At the same time, another image adds to the effect of the lamp lighting. From front to back, there's the text, the rounded light image, the lamp, and at the back, the light rays image.

*Figure 41. Lamp 3*

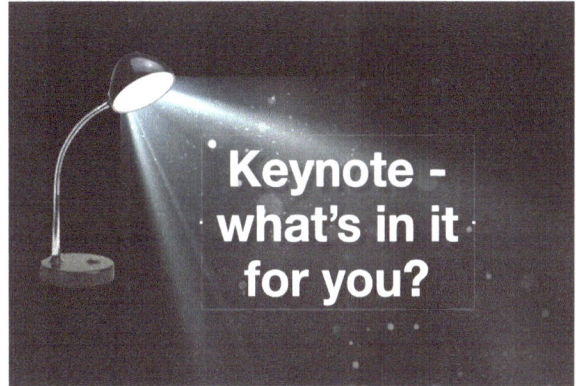

*Figure 42. Lamp 4*

Now the text is illuminated, so I overlay an exact copy of the text box, in exactly the same place, but in white. With all the timings right, one click lights the lamp, produces the light rays, and illuminates the title (Figure 42).

In this simple example, the lower part of the image is concealed by a black rectangle which blends with the black background.

*Figure 43. Library 1*

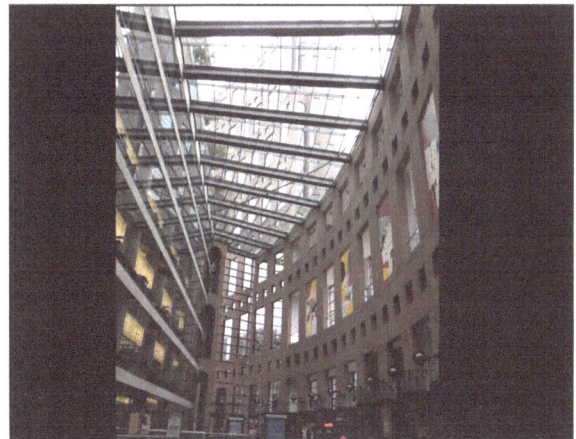

*Figure 44. Library 2*

On click, the rectangle dissolves to reveal the crowd using the space below. A similar technique could be used in this next example.

I needed to have a slow reveal of six bullet points. For text, the simplest way is to have all the text in a single text box, animate a dissolve, and set the text to appear on click, by paragraph. OR

Each of the six points could have been a separate object, dissolving in on click. OR On click, bullet point 1 could disappear, and bullet point 2 could appear, so that they show one by one.

I decided on a variation on the previous technique.

The text was covered over by six rectangles. In the screenshot below I've made them a different color, but in the presentation, they had to be the same as the background color.

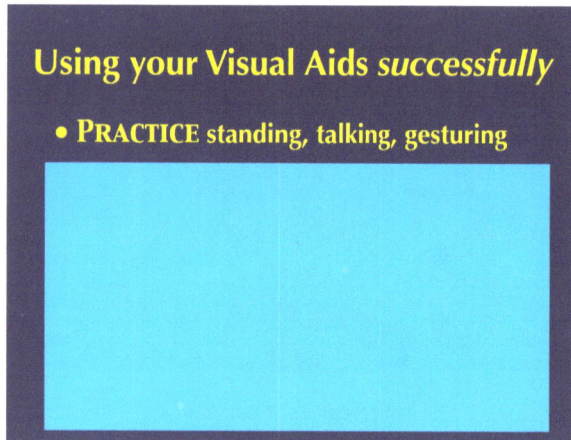

*Figure 45. Using Aids 1*

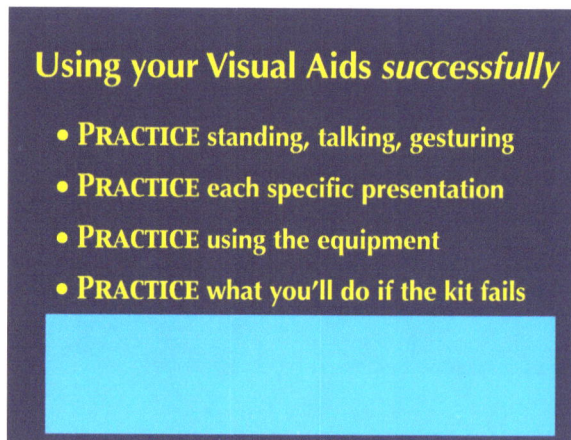

*Figure 46. Using Aids 2*

Select text, or a shape and then click on the color change icon. A useful facility in the color change box is that small symbol that looks like an eye dropper. Click on it, then on the color you want, anywhere you can find it on the screen. That selects the color, which is then applied to the text or shape. I used that to make sure the rectangles were all the same as the background.

On click, the first rectangle slowly dissolved (two seconds), revealing the first bullet point.

The next click dissolved the next rectangle, revealing the next bullet point, and so on.

There are several ways of achieving the same result. For text, it's easy to build the text in, bullet group by bullet group, on click. The reveal technique works for both text and images. It's a question of knowing what you want, and finding the technique that works best for you and your purpose. As with most things, master the basics and then move on to more advanced techniques.

### GIFs

You've seen GIFs — they're the little moving images on so many websites or text messages. A relevant GIF can be added to your presentation in the same way as any other image. As with any other effect, don't overuse it or the audience will tire and your purpose will be in jeopardy. Careful use of the techniques of build order/layering and overlays will certainly help you to create more impressive and more successful presentations, but we should be wary of spending time on it. Use it when you need it, not just because you can.

## 4.7 INFOGRAPHICS

There are entire books on infographics, because they are important. Any presentation can benefit from visuals and illustrations, and infographics will help an audience to understand numerical information. Good infographics are appealing, attention grabbing and memorable, and spreadsheets such as Excel and Numbers make it easy to generate pie charts, line and bar graphs in a variety of styles.

First, some general points. As with text, big and bold will work best. Use bright primary colors — red, yellow and blue — to catch attention. Keep it as simple as possible to make it easy for people to understand.

Next, decide which technique is appropriate for the data. We are used to seeing a line graph for temperature, because it is a continuous variable — the number can be anywhere, and the value changes smoothly from one to another. Car sales would be better as a bar graph because cars are sold as units — you can't buy half a car! The types of cars sold (sedans, SUVs, coupés) could be shown as a pie chart, with segments of the pie representing the different types of car. It isn't always easy to decide exactly which technique is best, but the guiding principle should be the purpose of the presentation. What does the audience need to know or understand to help achieve that purpose? What is the best way to present the data so that an audience can understand it ?

It is tempting to choose elaborate, high tech infographics, and they certainly have their place. A simple workplace presentation will benefit from simple, straightforward infographics.

Which of the following do you consider effective? Which might need the presenter to explain them? Or to put it another way, which would you be happy to include in your presentation? And for which audience might they be just right?

Figure 47. Asset values

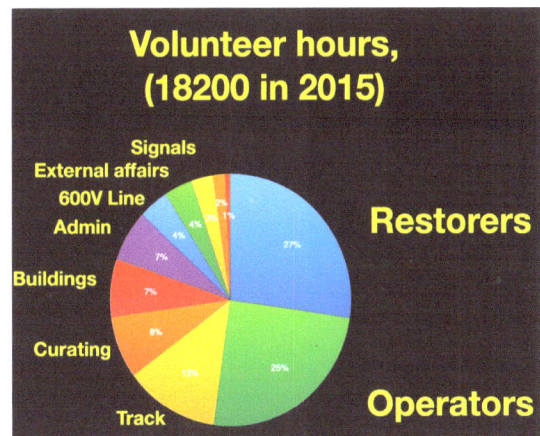

Figure 48. Volunteer Hours

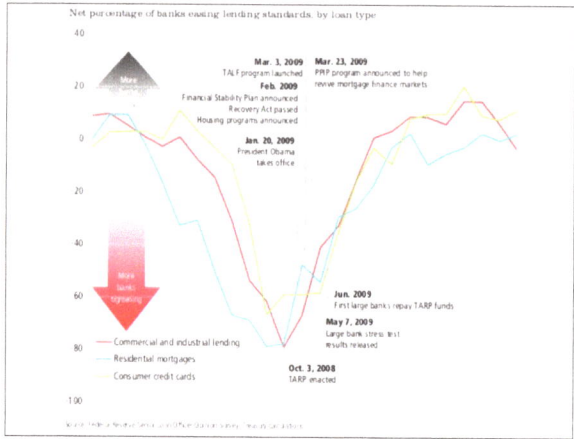

*Figure 49. Bank Loans*

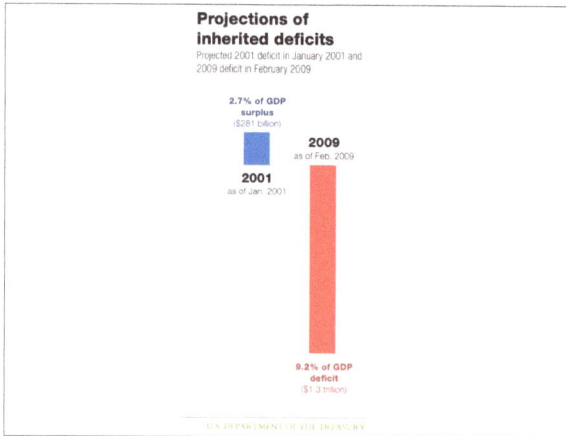

*Figure 51. Inherited Deficits*

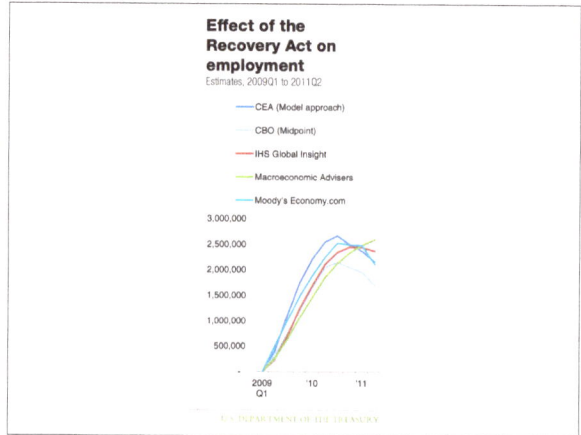

*Figure 50. Employment*

Preparing

# ❺
# Performing

## 5.1 MANAGING ANXIETY

**You can do this!**

I've been doing it for so long that it is very familiar, and as you gather presentation experience, you'll gain both confidence and expertise. Presentation skills, like any other, need practice. What is it about public speaking that makes it such an ordeal for so many? There seem to be several reasons.

- **Unfamiliarity:** for most people, public speaking is a relatively rare event, and so they experience anxiety over the unfamiliar.
- **Lack of confidence:** People often feel that others are more knowledgeable than they, or are better speakers.
- **Techno terror:** Will all the technology work as it should and will you remember all the routines, key presses and cues?
- **Sense of isolation:** When you rise to your feet, you're on your own. For many people who share office space and work in team units, that isolation is outside their normal comfort zone.
- **Audience intimidation:** The knowledge that there are "important people" in the audience can be intimidating to some.
- **The important occasion:** The presentation may be the key factor in getting a good grade or a job, winning agreement, committing capital to a new project or process, etc. Perhaps this

is why seasoned actors, used to working in front of an audience, suddenly find themselves tongue tied or babbling when they win an Oscar. (Or maybe they're just very good actors.)
- **Self-consciousness:** Because you're the focus of attention, you may feel particularly aware of your grammar, accent, voice quality, crumpled jacket, or image generally.
- **Fear of the fumble:** Standing there on your own, you feel that your errors will be exaggerated — a stumble over words, a misuse of vocabulary, the wrong graphic, etc.

### The Physical Effects of Anxiety

Anxiety prepares the body toward the "fight or flight" reaction: your heart rate picks up, breathing becomes a little quicker and adrenalin flow increases so that your reactions are faster than usual, and there's usually an increase in tension in the shoulder and neck area. All of these changes can affect your voice, making it sound a little higher pitched than usual, or leaving you breathless in the middle of a sentence, so that your delivery becomes disjointed. You're also thinking and reacting faster than usual, so you're more likely to pick up your pace and need to make a conscious effort to slow it down.

### What can you do about it?

The first good news is that you are not alone in this. Many experienced actors and radio and TV presenters experience this anxiety before "going on."

The second good news is that there are techniques you can use to help you handle this.

FIRST – THINK POSITIVE

Your anxiety is caused by a negative feeling of some kind. Think positive.

You will be successful.

The people in the audience are not intimidating. Most of them are just like you, and are in your corner.

The people in the audience are not intimidating. Most of them want to hear what you have to say.

Those "important people" in the audience are just ordinary people like you, and you can imagine them doing ordinary things such as brushing their teeth, reading the newspaper, or putting the cat out at night.

You won't fumble — you've prepared so well that you know you won't.

You may be away from your usual work team, but they're all on your side, and you can visualize them supporting you.

SECOND – PREPARE, AND PLAN

Knowing your stuff and knowing that you have a good plan (and a good backup plan) will help build your confidence.

THIRD – RELAX THE BODY

You might want to find a private space for this. If you're lucky there may be an anteroom you can use. Otherwise find the nearest toilet, and use a cubicle. Stand tall, take a deep breath, hold it, then breathe out slowly. At the same time try to relax your arms, shoulders and hands. Let them dangle loosely, and even shake them around gently. Repeat this as often as you can before you start to speak. With a little practice you can do this unobtrusively while waiting for the start.

Once, in a radio studio for an interview, before the start of the show the presenter mentioned that he had to complete his warmup routine. I sat back as he coughed and cleared his throat, flexed his arms and neck, and repeated some tongue twister phrases. With 10 seconds to go, he stopped and drew a couple of deep breaths. That worked for him. The red light went on, the mikes were live, and he began his introduction, smoothly and comfortably.

## FOURTH – RELAX THE VOICE

Loosen up your vocal cords with some simple exercises. Some like to run up and down a musical scale. If you're not a singer, try practicing a simple rhyme, on a rising pitch, and then on a descending pitch. As you recite the poem, exaggerate your mouth movements. Waggle the jaw around gently, to get the cheek and jaw muscles relaxed, and try a tongue-twister or two so that you concentrate on articulation and delivery.

## FIFTH – PRACTICE

You know the saying — practice makes perfect. It's true. Make a real effort to practice. In a traffic jam you can safely rehearse a talk, not just by running through it in your head, but by saying it out loud, just as you would in the real situation. (You may get some strange looks, but that's a small price to pay.)

Above all you must prepare for the presentation. Much of the fear and apprehension can be considerably lessened by a thorough preparation of the material to be presented, and by organizing your ideas into note form.

Jack Valenti, speechwriter for former President Lyndon Johnson, put it well when he said, *"The most effective antidote to stage fright and other calamities of speechmaking is total monkish preparation."*

For many people he's right, but not for all. You may be one of those who finds relaxation in activity. Your best way to relax might be to pace up and down a corridor, do a few stretch and bend exercises, run up and down a nearby staircase, or stroll around the car park.

Mark Twain also made a good point: "It usually takes more than three weeks to prepare a good impromptu speech." It's worth spending some time to find what works for you, and then make it part of your preparation / warmup routine.

You should also consider how you might handle questions. If you are detail-oriented, and meticulous in your planning, you might want to leave questions to the end so they don't interrupt your progress. If you are more comfortable with presentations, you might allow one or two during your delivery, but be careful not to be diverted from your purpose.

**When it all goes wrong**

One day it will. Most days everything will go as planned, but one day the power will fail, the connections won't connect, a critical bulb will blow, the screen will fall over, or any of a thousand other things will go wrong. Over the years I've had many things go wrong for me, and I know that despite all my planning and experience, it will happen again. It might be something minor, or it might not, and I've nearly always been able to find a way to deliver the presentation and achieve my purpose. (The two exceptions were the horror story in Section 8.1, and the occasion when I found myself in the ER instead of on my way to the venue.) It's always worth having a plan B, and for a more important occasion, perhaps even a plan C. Having a clear idea of your purpose will always help. You may not be able to achieve it the way you had planned, but what else can you do to achieve it? The way you handle adversity may make more of an impression on your audience than the presentation itself.

## 5.2 HELPING THEM OUT

**Help the person who has to introduce you to get it right.**

It's advisable to write your own introduction. The person doing introductions may be grateful for it, it's likely to take up less time, and your name is more likely to be pronounced properly. Having your own nameplate front and center will also help.

Please adapt this as needed to suit your own circumstances.

Date   /   /

| Title | Importance | Qualifications | Speaker | |
|---|---|---|---|---|
| Welcome to:… (speaker's name, with notes on pronunciation if necessary.) Title or topic is, | This topic is important because, | Our speaker today is well qualified because, | Please welcome, | Total time: 1 min |

*TABLE 5. SPEAKER INTRODUCTION*

## 5.3 WHO ARE THEY?

**They are the people you have to work with.**

It's important that you know some things about these people. You need to know because your presentation has a purpose, and to achieve it you have to relate to this audience. Knowing who they are makes it easier. If you have to persuade a colleague of something, and you know he or she is a keen golfer, you can perhaps work in a golfing analogy to make your point. It's less easy to relate to a group of people about whom you know nothing and that you see for the first time as you walk on to do your presentation.

Some presentations, such as a job interview, have a clearly defined audience and an equally clear purpose. Often the audience will be more varied, but whatever its size or composition, the more you know about them and their expectations the better.

A small audience may allow you to make it more personal by inviting individual responses — "Raise your hand if you agree/already know this/have experience with this." With small groups, especially workshops or training groups, it may be useful to provide nameplates for everyone so that you can address them by name.

A presentation to colleagues will usually have a clear purpose, and you're likely to know who to expect — the sales team, accountants, engineers, etc. Specialists such as these will be comfortable with their own specialist language (or jargon), and will expect you to use it.

Is your audience made up of decision makers? They will want precise information, and you can expect penetrating questions, so make sure your plan includes time for that.

Does your audience expect to be informed? You need to provide information in a clear and understandable format.

Do they need to be persuaded? You need to provide arguments, and perhaps allow discussion.

In a more general context, such as a conference, you can expect some level of common interest, but if there's an opportunity to mingle with the audience beforehand, take it. You can pick up accents, local concerns, particular interests and recent events. Some of this material could be worked into your presentation to give it greater local appeal, or just offer a little bonding.

I once spoke at a meeting where my presentation was preceded by a heated debate. As it happened, my presentation related to "Fire Festivals." I was able to start by remarking that I had thought my topic would be the most incendiary of the day. The laughter relaxed everyone and earned me a little more attention.

Clients too will have clear expectations to be met. The public will be more varied, but there is likely to be a common interest, e.g., the theme of the conference, or a specific topic. Rotarians and Lions can be expected to have an interest in community matters, and are likely to be keen to keep any talk to time so that they can get to, or back to, work.

Knowing what the audience wants is important if you are to achieve the purpose of your presentation.

What do they already know? It's important that you come in at the right level. Research is essential, and the more specialized the group, the more essential that is. A general public audience can understand that some of those present may have information gaps that need to be filled, or may need some basic background.

What experience do they already have? Find out, and you can build on it. Perhaps the experience is no more than knowledge of something that happened within the company or the community, and that shared experience can help you to bring everybody to a common understanding.

What does your audience need from you? Do they need new information or new ideas? Do they need increased understanding or motivation? Make sure that what you propose to achieve matches their need.

What is the audience goal for this presentation? Do they want to be enthused or convinced, informed or enlightened, motivated or inspired? Do not disappoint them. Make sure your purpose is as clear as possible, and that your presentation is designed to achieve that purpose.

There are three common life experiences that you can use in your presentation to help build a relationship with a varied audience. These are:

1. Family
2. Place
3. Work

Set a problem or a decision in a family context, and people can understand it and are more likely to remember it. If your audience is young, they are more likely to relate to a family situation involving young children. An older audience may be more familiar with issues involving teenagers, and senior citizens might be highly understanding of more complex family situations involving in-laws, family divorces, etc. The family situation could be theirs, yours, a TV family, or an imaginary one. An example could be decision making — how does your family decide on holiday destinations? That family experience, presented as a story, can make your point more memorable and help you achieve your purpose.

A local audience will usually react well to an appeal to local knowledge. You could refer to the main local traffic problem (everywhere seems to have at least one!), local landmarks or viewpoints, the local main street or mall, or a local festival or claim to fame. For a more diverse audience, try to find locations that are common to all. For a conference audience, that might be the venue, but you can also use the Statue of Liberty for Americans, the Eiffel Tower for the French, the Brandenberg Gate for Germans, etc. An example of how to use this might be about goals or pathways. Everybody knows where the Statue of Liberty/Tower of London/Eiffel Tower is, but can they tell you how to get there?

Work-based presentations lend themselves easily to work-related illustrations, especially those specific to the type of work an audience does, but even if the presentation is not about work, the workplace is a fruitful source of illustrations. Getting up in the morning, the Monday feeling, an interview with the boss, and Friday afternoon's sense of anticipation are common experiences that can be drawn upon. A presenter might want to make a point about motivation, and Monday morning and Friday afternoon can provide examples of differing motivation levels, and different motivating factors.

As mentioned elsewhere, stories can be powerful. A story about an individual and their specific motivation might be more effective than a general comment on motivation.


## 5.4 AUDIENCE SIZE

**A bigger audience is just a small audience on a larger scale.**

Sometimes the size of the audience is a cause for anxiety. If that applies to you, here are some thoughts that might help.

Think about the difference between a disc jockey (DJ) and a radio presenter. A disc jockey usually works with a crowd, and part of the task is to entertain and energize that crowd. Group techniques are an essential component of the toolbox — "Let's all clap hands."

The radio presenter may have a total audience of millions, but overwhelmingly, they are listening on their own. (Think of when *you* listen to the radio.) They might be in the car, out walking or jogging, or engaged in some task at home. They need to be addressed as individuals — "I hope you enjoy this too." When they hear someone saying "let's all do this" it doesn't feel right because they are on their own.

The most basic advice I ever heard was from a local politician who told me to — "talk to your audience, one person at a time." Nearly everybody is used to conversation with one other person, and the idea is that in your presentation you talk to a different person in the audience every few seconds, so you're talking to them in the familiar context of "one at a time." That takes away any trepidation you might have about presenting to a full auditorium. It certainly has been useful to me.

You might have to present to a small audience, in which case they all need to feel involved. Eye contact will be part of that. Keep looking around the group, leaving no-one out. Much the same applies as the audience grows. One presenter I saw kept his focus on the wall at the back of the room, above the audience. He never made eye contact with anyone, and the audience didn't feel involved. You can't look everyone in the eye, but the fact that you glance around to different places allows people to feel that you are involved with them.

It's important to understand that you are unlikely to be successful in reaching all of your audience, whatever its size. A small proportion will not be interested, swayed or persuaded, and there is little you can do about it. At the other end of the scale, a small proportion will think you are excellent and be fully with you. They need little further encouragement. The majority will be in the middle, and that is where you should direct your attention and energy, since that is where you will be most cost effective in trying to achieve your purpose.

## PA HORROR STORY

It was a hotel conference center, and the group was assembled to hear from an elected official about his area of expertise. He took the stage to applause, and the sound man duly turned up the gain on the stage microphone. The official grabbed the microphone and blew into it hard to see if it was working. In doing so he overloaded and blew the input stage of the sound system. Not content with committing the cardinal sin of maltreating the mike, the official promptly tried to blame the sound man, who despite this was able to reroute the signal and get going again.

PRESENTATION PURPOSE
– to impress audience

PROBLEMS
– poor microphone technique
– lack of courtesy toward the sound man

RESULT
– audience less than impressed

SOLUTIONS
– learn how to use a mike and PA system
– learn to trust the audio person

## 5.5 DO THEY TRUST YOU?

**Your presentation is better received if the audience trusts you.**
**Developing that trust can be achieved in a number of ways.**

If you have the opportunity to talk to any of the audience beforehand, say how much you appreciate the opportunity to present to them, and that you hope they will enjoy it. This also helps you to judge their needs, and perhaps even collect some local or topical information that you can use.

Do what you said you'd do in your presentation. If you have agreed on a title or theme for your presentation, be sure to stick to it. If your agenda or route map says you'll discuss X, Y and Z, then make sure that's what you do.

Be punctual. Arrive early for the presentation and stick as close to the specified time as you can. If you start 10 minutes late, don't just plow on regardless unless by prior arrangement with the organizers. In the context of a conference, you'll be remembered more positively as the one who finished on time than as the one who took your allocated time but made everyone late for lunch.

Wherever possible, write your own introduction, and write it with the specific audience in mind. Include any part of your expertise and experience that you think will help this specific audience to have confidence in you and trust you.

At times you'll be visible to the audience as you are introduced. If there are other presentations before yours, it's not just polite to show interest in the others — it's essential. Would you be interested in a presenter who had napped during somebody else's moment of glory?

Should you be "offstage" as you are being introduced, be sure to make an entrance. That doesn't mean a showbiz entrance., but you should try to walk on with confidence, knowing where everything is, and where to place anything you are carrying. Think of the alternative. Would you be ready to pay attention to someone who shuffles into view, can't find the lectern, and has to search for a place to lay his notes?

Be professional, competent and accurate. Make sure you have the facts, the correct spelling of names, processes, job titles, etc.

Be relevant. For example, use local references or incidents to make a point to a general audience. Use work-based references if talking to staff, travel references if talking to travel professionals, etc.

Look at your audience, especially when you're making a key point. Make eye contact with as many of them as you can by making sure you look at different parts of the room, not just at the same one or two people.

Be honest about your knowledge and expertise. In particular, admit to uncertainty or lack of knowledge when that applies, or to a margin of error in any statistics. Suggest better authorities, or indicate a willingness to research a point and get back to a questioner.

Be aware that people make decisions with both hearts and minds. The balance of those two is often heavily in favor of one or the other, and sometimes neatly balanced. If you can assess which factor is more likely to be more significant, you'll be better able to select appropriate stories and design your presentation to achieve your purpose.

Acknowledge the needs of the audience. If they are dealing with change, recognize the progress they've made. If they have to make a difficult decision, sympathize with their dilemma.

Use audience engagement techniques. These are simple ways of involving your audience. With any size of audience, invite them to share. "Don't you agree?" said while looking at them and nodding your head encourages them to do exactly that, and to feel more empathy toward you.

With small groups where you can easily reach the recipient, a simple gift (a happy face badge, a pencil or pen) to reward a good question will work. Small groups can also introduce themselves without taking up much time, or participate in a brief quiz, or be involved by standing up, raising hands, etc. Small groups will also respond to an arrival gift of your business card and a pen. Handing these out one by one is more effective than placing them on the tables beforehand.

For larger audiences, try an early show of hands on some topic-related question, especially along the lines of 'How many think this will be of use to you?'. A willing volunteer from the audience can be used in a suitable role play, or write notes on a flip chart, be a timekeeper, etc. Be sure to give them a good reward, e.g., a bottle of wine or a box of chocolates. If the presentation requires group discussion, make sure you have groups at tables, have each table appoint a spokes-person, and give them enough time, but not too much.

Other engagement techniques include the use of pictures, props, and the range of presentation aids as discussed in Section 2.4.

The guiding principle for selection is always, "How will this help to achieve the purpose?"

## 5.6 SAYING WHAT YOU SAY AND THE WAY THAT YOU SAY IT

**Talk is just part of what you have to do.**

When people think of a presentation, they nearly always think of a talk. Sometimes, especially for a short presentation, speech may be all that is needed. For longer presentations, it can become more important to consider other techniques that will help to make your point and achieve your purpose.

**Composition**

A good start is a welcome message. You can use it to check the focus of a projected image, but it could also be a flip chart page standing slightly to one side. The benefit is that it helps set the tone for your presentation.

Getting the structure right — the title, body and conclusion — is half the battle. Before you dash off to put pen to paper, or digits to keyboard, remember that you're going to be speaking. What you are about to write isn't an essay. It has to be the spoken word. Read an essay out loud and it rarely works. Sit down to read through a speech and it doesn't always work too well either.

An essay can use more complicated grammar and vocabulary because they present little difficulty for the reader, but can be stumbling blocks for verbal delivery. Tongue-twisters rarely present an obstacle to the eye.

A speech, robbed of pace, intonation and character, can feel flat when read. I've watched a number of high school events where the winner of an essay competition was required to read their essay to the assembled crowd. So often, the reader looked and sounded uncomfortable, because they had written an essay, not a script.

You know yourself and whether you are more comfortable with a fully written script, or a series of notes. Practice will tell you when you have it right. Pay particular attention to unfamiliar vocabulary or tongue-twisters. In any presentation, simpler language is easier to deliver and will generally be easier for the audience to understand.

Think carefully about the overall presentation, and its purpose. How will your presentation flow? Start with just enough preliminary information to make it clear what you are talking about, and why. Be clear and explicit at the beginning, including a quick outline and an indication of what makes your talk interesting. Your audience might wander off if they can't see early on that there's a good reason to stay.

Don't waste much time on preliminaries; you might run out of time before getting to the juicy stuff and session chairs are notoriously strict about enforcing the schedule. Put the interesting stuff in the middle of the talk, where it belongs. Save the "boring" stuff (apologies for unfinished implementations, long lists of related work, variations and future work) for the end.

Don't feel compelled to justify every minor statement during the main part of the talk; you have presumably justified them in your research. If people challenge you during the question period, you can make your justifications then. Of course, don't leave your most important or controversial statements unjustified.

Your topic might be one about which you are passionate. Sometimes you can use that passion. It might help if your purpose is to persuade, but might not be as useful or relevant if your primary purpose is to inform.

Keep your summary and conclusions brief. Don't recapitulate all the points made in the talk; emphasize the main ideas that you want the audience to remember. If you run out of time, skip the summary and conclusions slide, since it doesn't say anything new.

Consistency of projected images is important. PowerPoint/Keynote presentations work best with landscape-oriented images, since laptop and TV screens are built that way. Overhead Projector (OHP) images can be either, but portrait works best.

Here are some example Keynote slides that might help.

## 2    Stay out of the picture

Stay facing the audience, and in contact with them.

Stay to the side of the projector, so that you don't block the light.

Point with your mouse, not on the screen.

## 3   Let it be square

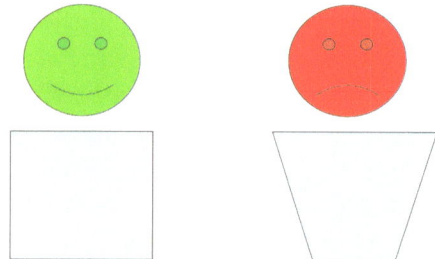

Avoid 'keystoning'

*Figure 52. Out of picture*

*Figure 53. Keystoning*

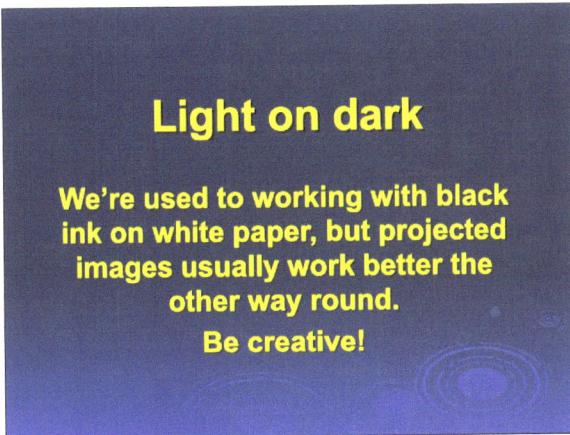
Figure 54. Light on Dark

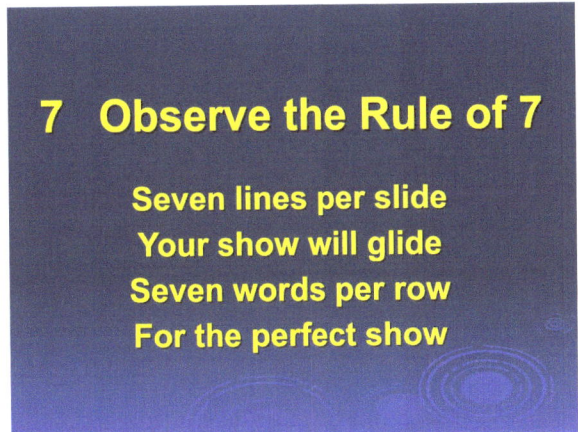
Figure 55. Rule of Seven

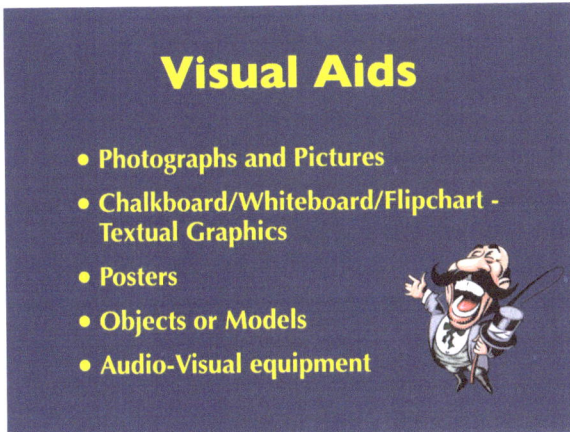
Figure 56. Visual Aids

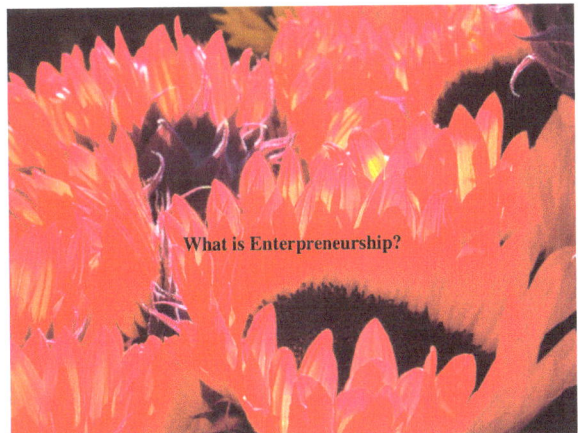
Figure 57. Entrepreneurship

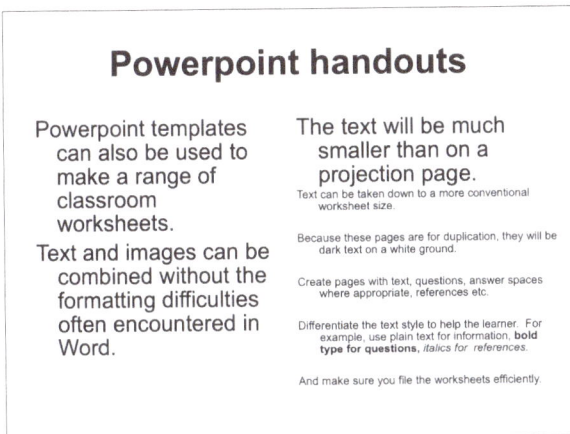
Figure 58. Powerpoint Handouts

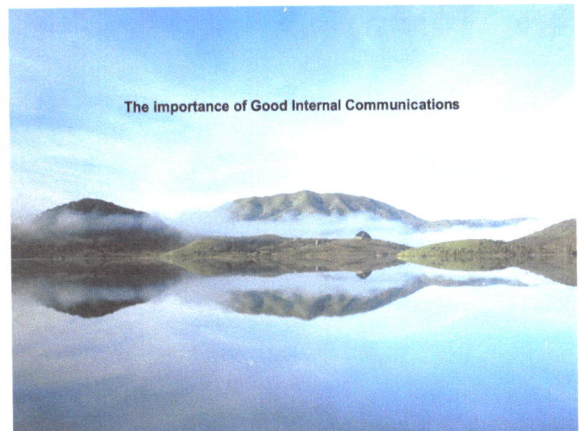
Figure 59. Good Internal Communications

As you'll see in the above slides, not all styles work. Your task may be easier if there is a corporate style or template for you to follow, but otherwise you have control over the color and style selections for your presentation. Choose wisely, always remembering your purpose.

The horror stories scattered throughout this book are reminders that not everyone plans or prepares properly, or makes careful or appropriate selections of aids, or even of personnel to do the presentation.

## 5.7 LISTENING

**Your audience speaks to you.**

It was an army training sergeant who challenged us. Concealment was the theme of the day, and we had been heaving nets and branches around to make our vehicles invisible to the casual passerby.

"OK gentlemen," he said, "we've hidden ourselves from the eyes. Now we hide from the ears."

He made us stand and listen. The training ground was a quiet rural area, and we could hear the whisper of the wind in the grass, the rustle of leaves, the creak of swaying branches, the occasional birdsong, and the faint hum of traffic on a distant road.

"There's a hidden word in 'Listen,'" pronounced the sergeant. "What is it?"

It took a couple of minutes for it to dawn on us, but it was so obvious when we got it. The word is 'silent.'

To us, the lesson was that camouflage was pointless unless we could stay quiet too. To a presenter, the lesson is that to listen, you have to be silent. Think about that for a moment. For much of this book we're considering what the presenter will say, but the audience also speaks, and has to be heard.

You'd be tempted to think that we're going to look at questions, and we will, but any audience speaks in more than one way, and questions are simply the most obvious of these.

An audience speaks to you even before you stand up. Is the audience quiet and attentive, eager and expectant, or restless, inattentive, bored and disinterested? The signs are there to be read. Positive signs are that they look at you, make eye contact, nod in agreement, and stay quiet. Negative signs include restless stirring in seats, frequent glances at windows and wristwatches, rustling as papers are shuffled and consulted, and a general wilting of posture as people sink and hunch down into their seats. It's as important to 'listen' for these symptoms as it is to listen carefully to any questions that are asked. But what do you do when you hear them?

Part of the answer is that if you've taken care of the planning stage properly, your presentation will be so interesting and attention grabbing, that the audience will be riveted from the start. In truth, no matter how well you prepare, and no matter how famous or experienced you might be, eventually there will be an audience which tells you it isn't listening anymore. How do you recover the situation, and get back on track? Do you have any 'audience retrieval' techniques up your sleeve?

A lecture I once attended was held in a hotel conference room, with the warm sunshine outside, and deep comfortable chairs. I could feel myself drifting, and sensed that others were too. The lecturer noticed, and gently nudged a heavy book off his lectern. It hit the floor with a thump, startling the drowsy and refocusing our attention on the matter at hand. A bit dramatic perhaps, but as an audience retrieval technique it worked.

Another occasion was rescued more inadvertently. The speaker was losing us, but didn't know it. He had a low and monotonous delivery, and the room was sultry. At one point he turned to one side, took a pace forward, caught his foot in a chair leg, and staggered forward for several paces before finally crashing to the floor. He was unhurt, and it took some minutes before he could resume, but when he did, it was to a fully awake audience.

A more professional recovery was the case of the speaker who sensed that his audience was increasingly elsewhere. He had already shown a number of slides, and was about to move to the next.

"I think this point is best illustrated on my next slide," he said, "which just happens to be of my recent visit to the White House."

He pretended to fumble with the slide, while the audience gathered itself in sudden anticipation. The slide came on, and was a conventional graph.

"Ah — the wrong slide — but a useful one nevertheless since it ..."

Of course it was never intended to be anything else, but the remark did the trick for him. He had listened to his audience, sensed the drift and taken steps to regain everybody's attention.

It's a repeatable ploy, and a handy one to have tucked away in the toolbox. You need an apparently innocuous or outrageous remark up your sleeve.

Examples include:

*"Last week my nephew told me he'd bought three new hotels."*

*Pause*

*"He's getting really good at Monopoly."*

*"By the way, have you heard that the Rolling Stones/Queen Latifah/the President will be in town next week?"*

*Pause*

*"I just wish I knew which town."*

A regular presenter will find it useful to have a few of these 'audience retrieval' techniques in their repertoire.

At question time, the listening skill comes more obviously into play. You have three things to listen to.

1. the questioner's words
2. the questioner's other agenda
3. the audience reaction

In preparing your presentation, it's useful to try to anticipate questions that an audience might have. You can't always get it right but it's safe to assume that someone will want to see a graphic again, so it helps to have them arranged so that you can go back to a specific one if necessary. Aren't you glad you did that flip chart index?

With PowerPoint you've probably seen a presenter turn back to the start and work down the list of slides to find the right one. It's useful to go back to that key image, but remember to blank the projector while you do it. Don't show your underware!

Make sure that you understand the question. You can repeat a short question, paraphrase a longer one. This has two other advantages. First, it gives you a little time to think. Second, it helps to make sure that the audience members all hear the question.

Questioners tend to fall into several recognizable categories. Perhaps you've been one of these at some time?

The straightforward question is the one you welcome. Somebody is interested and wants some more information or background, and all you have to do is provide it. You owe it to the questioner to give a fair answer, and to the audience to be reasonably brief so that you move on to the next question.

The Earnest questioner is usually a left-brain type, who likes things clearly explained and properly identified. Expect to be questioned on the detail of something you've said or shown. Provided that you know your subject matter (and you should) these are easy questions to answer, but have an ear for the audience. They might become restless if you dwell on the answer too long, or if the questioner gets in with one or two supplementary questions.

The Expert Questioner isn't really asking you for further information, but wants to demonstrate his or her own credibility in the subject area. The question is often of the form "Don't you agree that?" This questioner would love to become involved in debate, and so that's the last thing you should do. Agree or disagree as quickly and simply as you can, thank them for their interesting question or viewpoint, and move on.

The Challenger doesn't believe something you said, or disagrees with it and wants to take issue with you. Sometimes it's a neutral challenge because of the questioner's doubt, or it can be a hostile challenge because you are contradicting a well-held position. Again you have to listen to the audience. Sometimes their restlessness will tell you straight away that this is a familiar scenario, that your challenger is known, and that they've heard it all before. If so, you can readily thank the questioner, give a brief answer, suggest that this is an area that merits much detailed discussion, and you'll be happy to meet them afterwards for that purpose. The audience will also tell you it's a neutral challenge, to which they may be apathetic, or they hush and listen, indicating that they too want this one answered. So do it, as accurately and dispassionately as you can.

The Rambler doubtless knows what the question is, but has to lead into it gently, precede it with preamble, and surround it in verbal clothing. There may be a pearl of a question in there, but it is hard to see. Wait for a suitable opportunity, and say as firmly and clearly as you can, "So let me just be clear about what your question is."

If that doesn't work, you probably have to thank them for an interesting point, wish there was time to answer it now, offer to answer it later over coffee, and hope that they don't follow up on the offer.

While answering questions, it's important to remember the purpose of your presentation and your role within the organization. If you're a "visiting" presenter, it's clearly no part of your purpose to offend anyone in the audience — that's not in your agreement, and it's unlikely to endear you to those who hired you. Remember that in any business, it's usually easier to hold on to an existing client than to find a new one!

If you're tackling something within your own organization, it's reasonable to expect that somebody in your audience might feel a ruffled feather and perhaps become a Challenger or an Expert (especially if they felt they should have been doing the presentation instead of you!). However tempting it might be to score a point or inflict a putdown, you should resist it. Is alienation of your colleagues, or weakening of team relations a part of your remit? Instead, you should use the presentation not just to resolve the question, but also to strengthen relationships and improve teamwork.

Anticipate questions: Think of the two most likely questions and plan your answers.

Understand the question: Paraphrase it if necessary, repeat it if needed.

Plan the answer, particularly if you anticipated the question.

Do not digress. Politicians often do that, but you need to stick to the topic.

Be honest: If you can't answer the question, say so — you can offer to find out and provide an answer later.

Control interchanges: If a questioner becomes a heckler or digresses, try to remind the audience of the goal of the presentation. "You're certainly very keen on that point, and I'd be happy to talk with you about it later, but do we all want to stay with this or move on?"

Use the last question of the day to summarize, and remind your audience of the purpose of the presentation. "On that note, I hope you've learned what you need to know about this new plan, and are ready to go out there and put it into action, and to reap its benefits."

Indicate your availability. You're there to provide a total package of service and after-care. You can stay behind should anyone wish to talk to you. You'll be able to answer other questions over coffee. Have business cards available for follow-up. Invite people to write questions on the back of their business card and have a clearly labeled jar or box in which to collect them. Make sure that any questions that you collect are answered.

**AUDIENCE HORROR STORY**

The speaker was introduced, rose, and walked to the lectern. With only a brief glance at the audience, the presenter launched forth and read carefully written notes. It sounded formal and stilted, because it had been written to be read rather than heard. The reading demanded such attention that only occasionally was there time for the presenter to look up, and then only for the briefest time. The audience felt ignored, lost interest, and wondered why they couldn't have been given a copy of the speech to read for themselves.

PRESENTATION PURPOSE
– to engage and inform audience

## THE PROBLEM
– poor technique, failing to engage the audience

## RESULT
– audience not engaged, only partly informed

## SOLUTIONS
– engage the audience
– rehearse, use notes, use a planner

## 5.8 SPEAKING BODY LANGUAGE

### The Hidden Message

If you're visible before you speak, people will look at you, out of curiosity if nothing else. However you feel, it will help to appear calm and confident. Look around the audience if you feel comfortable doing that, otherwise skim over your notes, or pretend to do so. Think about it. If you appear nervous and uncertain, the audience will be losing confidence in you, will begin to anticipate a poor performance, and will be less likely to listen to you. Put on a show of confidence, and they are more likely to give you their serious attention.

When you stand up, you can convey a range of messages, probably without meaning to. Moving around suggests a restlessness that your audience is likely to pick up. One way to counter this is to adopt a comfortable neutral stance. Neutral means standing with your arms hanging naturally at your side, balanced on legs slightly apart. It isn't too easy, especially if your inclination is to move around, wave your arms, and gesticulate.

One of the best examples I know of the neutral stance is Patrick Stewart in the role of Captain Picard of the Starship Enterprise. Watch him, and you'll see that he usually stands in neutral, so that when a gesture is called for it has effect. He also walks with his arms hanging loosely by his side. Try it, and it will feel unnatural, but it is worth practicing.

An alternative is to integrate your moving. Use a pause to move to another position. Move when you are talking about a process or a continuation, i.e., while saying "on and on and on" or "etc., etc., etc."

The main thing is to keep yourself within what is comfortable for you. Try to avoid being confined to a static position (e.g., behind a lectern) if your natural style is to prowl. You might want to restrict your movement if it conveys restlessness, or wave your arms less if it becomes distracting. Limiting your movement, or reducing your arm waving is more achievable than trying to eliminate it.

Alternatively, if you prefer to be static, you might want to include a little movement to help maintain audience attention. Use some movement to punctuate the presentation. Even just shifting your balance to the other side can be used to empathize a change of direction, a new topic, or a new factor. Tweaks are easier to achieve than rebuilds.

## 5.9 WHAT TO DO WITH YOUR HANDS

**Hands – A Distraction, or a Tool**

Watch people talk, and you'll quickly see that many use their arms and hands to punctuate and embellish what they say. Such movements may already be a natural part of your style, but they are usually too vague to be useful in the context of a presentation. Presentation gestures need to be purposeful and planned, exaggerated and held. Gestures that are part of a constant kaleidoscope of gesticulations lose their effectiveness. This is where the neutral stance plays its part. A gesture that starts from a neutral stance, and is followed by a neutral stance, has more effect. There are some standard gestures that you can use, and you may develop others to suit your purpose. Hint — TV preachers are usually quite good at this. Observe TV preachers with the sound turned down, and learn.

Everyone: Raise your right arm across your body to shoulder height, point to the left, and with palm almost upwards, sweep slowly to the right. Hold the gesture as long as you can.

Me: Hands flat, middle fingers of each hand in to the chest.

You: Don't use your index finger to point. Stretch your arms out forward, thumbs uppermost, and spread the fingers a little. Move the arms outward a little to include those sitting to the sides.

High: Raise one hand as high as you can, and flatten down the fingers as though placing them on a shelf. Tilt the upper body slightly to get the arm truly vertical, and to emphasize the gesture.

Higher and higher: Similar gesture, but done in three or four stages, starting at chest height. Make sure each stage is a clean, abrupt change from the previous one. Alternatively, hold your fists to the front and pile one on top of the other, or start low inside and take your hand diagonally up and to the outside (do it the other way, and you end up with your arm across your face).

Grasp opportunity: A sweeping movement forward and upwards, starting with an open hand, finishing with a clenched fist at shoulder height.

Advance: A horizontal version of "higher."

Open out: Start with hands held out in front, palms together. Draw them apart slowly, but end with arms horizontal and palms open and upward, fingers spread.

Practice in front of a mirror. Your gestures may look and feel uncomfortably exaggerated, but they'll work in a presentation. Learn to make them clear, and to hold them. As with any aid, gestures reinforce the message, so use them when and where you need to and try to stay "neutral" in between.

Presentation gestures are really just an exaggerated version of what you might normally do, so in planning your presentation, let yourself react naturally to the words and pick out where you would normally gesture. Build on the most effective of those, so that you are doing what comes naturally, but adding to it. At the same time, try to stay neutral in between, so that when you do gesture, it works.

Make your gestures succeed. The list above has gestures that are easy to understand, and complement what you are saying. A gesture opportunity has to include a purposeful gesture, and you may have to design and practice using it so that it becomes fluid and natural.

A gesture should be convincing. A half-hearted gesture is in the same league as a half-drawn graphic or a half-completed sentence. It has to be lively, distinct, and vigorous, but slow enough to let your audience follow it. Practice in front of a mirror.

In making a gesture, you go through three distinct phases. Let's consider the gesture for "high" from the list above. Start in neutral, but your body begins to adjust to the forthcoming movement. Reach your cue and your arm rises, your shoulder tilts, the hand reaches, and the fingers come together before flattening to the horizontal. Hold the gesture for as long as needed, and bring the arm down, stand straight, and return to neutral.

Those three stages of Readiness, Execution, and Return give the gesture a flow, making it smooth and effective. Avoid making gestures that snap from phase to phase like a soldier on the parade ground. A smooth flow is important. A half-hearted gesture that jerks from phase to phase will be worse than no gesture at all.

Achieving smooth and effective gestures may be the hardest part of all this, because it'll feel the least natural part of a presentation. You can improve your gesturing capability by developing mini gestures in conversation, which you can work up into full gestures for presentation purposes. Observe gestures that other people use, and use any that suit your purpose. You may also have to do some work to minimize the distracting mannerism or the ineffectual gesture. Practice recording yourself on video, or in front of a trusted (and properly briefed) family member or colleague.

You might also find it useful to watch some YouTube hosts in action, and observe their use of gestures, how they hold their heads, maintain eye contact, etc.


## DELIVERY HORROR STORY

A group presentation was arranged as part of a workshop. On cue, the group made their way, in carefully managed order, to the prescribed area. The first ones to arrive were shuffled to the back as the others arrived, and once all were ready, the first person to speak had to fight their way through the group to get to the front.

PURPOSE
– to convey the result of the group's collective thinking

PROBLEM
– failure to think through delivery of presentation

RESULT
– group's thinking not received as well as it might have been

SOLUTION
– plan presentation to include all elements of delivery

# ❻
# Being Practical

*Practical – preparing the script, aids, equipment and other resources that might be needed.*

## 6.1 USING VISUAL AIDS

**The right visual aids can make all the difference.**

Aids are intended to augment your presentation, and help your audience to understand and enjoy it so that you achieve your purpose. The most basic thing to remember is that the best technology available to you is yourself. You are more versatile, more flexible, and more impressive than anything else. You are the one designing and delivering this presentation, and are the core of it. Any aids you bring to bear are just that — aids, not substitutes or replacements.

Once you have a plan for your presentation, consider the various audio and visual aids that you might use to make sure you get your message across and fulfill your purpose.

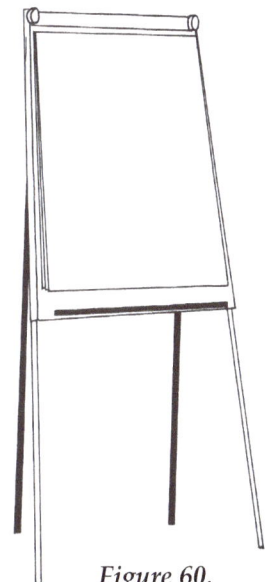

*Figure 60.*
*Flipchart Easel*

*Visual aids can*
- Enhance understanding
- Add authenticity
- Add variety
- Help the speaker build ethos (speaker credibility)
- Help engage the audience
- Help your presentation achieve its purpose

## General Principles

Make sure the visual aid supplements the presentation rather than becoming the presentation itself. A visual aid should be like a good actor, offstage until needed, on stage to play its part, and offstage afterwards. (If it isn't in use — it's underware.)

- *Emphasis:* should emphasize what the presentation emphasizes
- *Relevance:* should be relevant to the presentation or to the point being made
- *Simplicity:* should be simple, and easy to understand
- *Balance:* should be balanced and pleasing to the eye
- *Color:* adds effect to graphics

## Using Your Visual Aids Successfully

- Practice. Make sure any visual aid is integrated into your presentation.
- Plan the placement of any visual aid before the presentation.
- Check to see that your electronic equipment is running, and that you know how to properly operate it.
- Do not display it until you are ready to use it. When finished with it, remove or cover it. (*Don't show your underware.*)
- Do not stand directly in front of it, stand to the side and face the audience.
- When referring to the Visual Aid, point, don't leave your audience searching.
- Do not distribute materials during your presentation. If you have prepared handouts, distribute them before or after you speak.

## Varieties of Visual Aids

- People: body, clothes, grooming, actions, gestures, voice, facial expressions, and demeanor
- Sketches, cartoons, etc.
- Maps
- Graphs:
    - Pie or circle, to show parts of a whole
    - Bar, to show discrete variables
    - Line, to show continuous variables
- Charts:
    - Flowchart, to show a process such as production
    - Tree, to show hierarchies

- Sequence, to show steps in order
- Pictographs
- Photographs and pictures – make sure they are high resolution
- Whiteboard: text and graphics
- Posters
- Objects or models
- Audio-visual equipment
- Handouts
- Video
- Audio

## 6.2 USING STORIES

### A good story can be a great asset

You may be able to harness the power of a story in your presentation to help you achieve your purpose. If dealing with "Internal Communications" tell the story of a single message as it travels through the system. Or the story of a single customer dealing with your company, or the ways in which different individuals value different aspects of your business. If appropriate, the entire presentation could be a story.

Stories involving emotion are especially powerful. I once heard parents telling the story of their daughter's death due to a drug overdose. Their audience was several hundred teenagers. As they told the story of their loss, you could have heard a pin drop. Every teenager imagined their own parents coping with a comparable situation. I had the feeling that even those who thought their own parents didn't love them, sat sympathizing with their peers whose parents did.

Another powerful story came from a Rotarian who told the story of a woman's life as a widow raising a child. The woman had run into financial trouble and been helped by the local Rotary Club. A few years later, when her financial state improved, she became a Rotarian. She then revealed that this was her own story, and thus was hugely effective in drawing attention to the plight of single mothers.

Your story might be one of overcoming odds, of reaching a goal or of participating in some great adventure, occasion, or team event. Have you canoed down the Colorado? Attended a presidential inauguration? Been a member of a championship team? Or do you know a friend who has? Sometimes a familiar historical figure or event can be your story, using its familiarity to remind us, or draw a parallel. The story might also be the story of an ordinary person doing an ordinary thing. Perhaps you need to invoke the image of the ordinary customer for a product or service, or the worker at a specific stage in a production or supply chain process.

A good story lets the listener imagine being in the same situation, and wondering how they might react to it. It's an excellent way of involving an audience, but you have to be a good storyteller and that might need some practice.

Good stories linger in the memory long after they are told. It may not always be appropriate, but where possible, and when it helps achieve your purpose, try to give your audience a story that touches a chord, appeals to their emotions, or sets out a situation with which all can empathize.

## 6.3 HELPING YOUR VOICE

**You wouldn't give your audience an out of focus image.**
**Make sure any audio in your presentation is equally clear.**

It is one of the curiosities of life that nobody ever asks if the cameras are in focus, but few people can resist the temptation to check the sound system, if only by asking if everyone can hear them. If preparation has been done properly, you know the system works and can simply step up to the mike and start talking.

Larger venues will almost certainly have a public address system or PA, and someone to help you set it up for best Front of House (FOH) sound, i.e., the sound the audience will hear. You don't necessarily have to know how to operate it, but you do have to know how to use it.

### MICROPHONE HORROR STORY

The presenter pulls the microphone up close and talks intimately into it. You are bombarded with every click of the teeth, every gurgle of saliva, every wind rush of inhalation and exhalation. Sibilant 's' sounds screech at you, and the explosions of p, b, and t sounds browbeat you into submission. By the end you know you're exhausted, and remember vividly and permanently how it was said, but have little memory of what was said.

PRESENTATION PURPOSE
– to engage and inform audience

THE PROBLEM
– poor mike technique

RESULT
– audience minimally engaged, partly informed

SOLUTIONS
– don't get too close to a mike
– listen to your audience

**Here are a few DOs and DON'Ts:**

| DO | DON'T |
|---|---|
| Arrange the mike so that it is in front of and just below your mouth — about 15 cm or six inches away — when you stand to speak. | Leave the positioning until the moment when you stand up to speak. |
| Check the system beforehand so you know it works. | Blow into the mike to see if it works. |
| Make an opening remark and then ask if everyone can hear you clearly. | Assume that because the system is on, they can all hear you. |
| Have someone available to make any adjustments, and leave them to do it for you | Try to make adjustments yourself, unless there is no alternative. |
| Stop immediately if there is a problem such as feedback howl, or severe distortion. | Plow on through an obvious and severe problem. |
| Abandon the system if you have to, and try to speak clearly and a little more loudly. | Press on regardless. |
| Try to stay the same distance from the mike so the audience has a consistent sound level to work with. | Rock back and forth, or from side to side as you speak. |
| Move away from the mike when you finish — it's a visual cue to the audience, and a precaution against broadcasting sighs of relief! | Mutter quietly to yourself in front of an open or live mike. |

*TABLE 6*

### Microphones

Most microphones are fairly robust, and it's fair to assume that any mike on a stage is directional. That means it picks up sound more from one direction than another — usually the direction it points in, or the front.

Whatever the mike, it pays to know how to use it. Your voice is going to be the mainstay of your presentation, so having it heard clearly is crucial.

The most common fault is speaking too close to the mike, as in the horror story above. This gives a muffled and muddied sound that can be hard to listen to, yet I've heard more than one speaker profess to like it that way. Those same speakers would never dream of using an out-of-focus picture, but seem happy to give their audience the audio equivalent.

The second most common fault is moving away from the mike, usually to the side, which means the mike picks up less well. Maintaining a consistent position helps.

If presentations are to be a regular part of your life, it might be worth investing in your own microphone. There are many to choose from, but here are one or two suggestions.

First, a handheld mike. Not that you would be advised to hold it in your hand, but this type can also be placed on a stand. The two mikes you see at any US presidential lectern are Shure SM57s. The SM57 uses a standard XLR connector, and XLR cables can be easily joined to reach a mixing deck or PA system. If they're good enough for the president, they should suit you, and next time you see a presidential press conference, notice where they are placed. You'll also note that on presidential lecterns (apart from 45), the mikes are low down. This is partly so that the photographers have a clear view, and partly to reduce distortion and plosives.

Plosives are the p, b, f and t sounds that involve a rush of air as you pronounce them, especially when you're trying to project your voice. Hold your hand in front of your mouth as you say, "Peter bought a proper boat," and you can feel the air movement. Microphones can be overloaded by this and the result is a popping sound that is not too pleasant for the listener. Avoid this by not taking directly into the mike. If you have to talk close to a mike, talk over the top of the mike. Use a windshield or wind muff whenever possible. Most foam windshields don't help much, so if you invest in your own mike, consider a "furry" for it. A furry windshield does a much better job, and except on the calmest of days, is essential if you are working outside.

A handheld mike occupies one hand, which might not be a problem, and a stand-mounted mike means you have to stay in one place. This might be useful if you are on camera in a televised or streamed presentation, or are participating in a video conference, but it can be an impediment if you are a natural mover and pacer.

Second, a lapel or tieclip mike. These mikes are small and unobtrusive, and leave your hands completely free. The Sennheiser ME2 is a good example, but its cable ends in a 3.5mm jack since it's intended to plug into a small body pack wireless transmitter. If you buy any tieclip mike, make sure you also buy an adaptor or connector to allow you to plug into XLR inputs. Tieclip mikes are best placed in the center of your chest, and you might notice a little drop off in volume when you turn your head to the side. Since the mike is placed well below your mouth a windshield isn't usually necessary unless you are outside. Figure 61 (above) shows a foam windshield to the left of the mike, and a furry to the right.

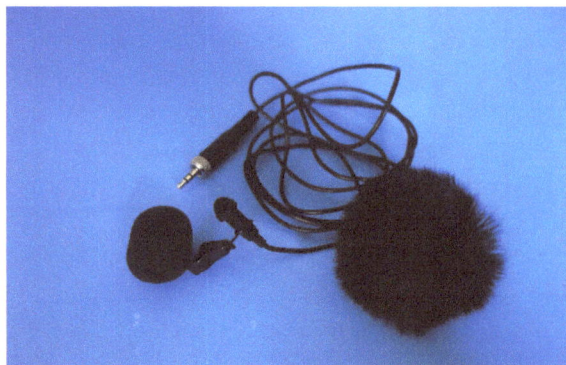

*Figure 61. Tieclip mike with windshields*

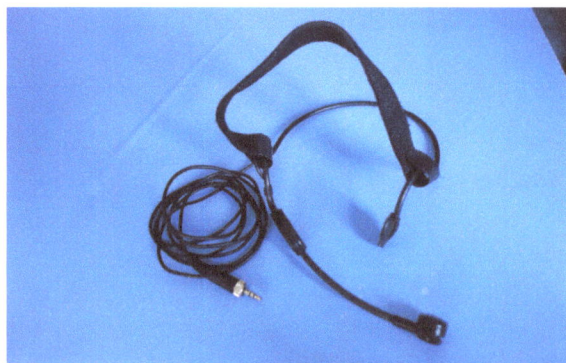

*Figure 62. Headset Mike*

Third, a headset (Figure 62). This involves a headband support and a small boom that places a mike close to your mouth, and slightly to one side so as to avoid the plosive sounds. Add a furry if necessary. The advantage is that you can move your head freely, and be sure of a consistent sound volume. The Sennheiser ME3 is one of many quality headsets available. It too terminates in a 3.5mm jack for the body pack wireless transmitter.

Tieclip and headset mikes particularly lend themselves to wireless operation. A wireless mike gives you freedom of movement on the stage or podium if that is important.

If choosing a wireless mike, go to a reputable store that specializes in audio equipment, and be prepared to pay for professional quality equipment. It's worth it in the long run. Take into consideration where you might be using it. Sennheiser and Shure publish frequency finder sites. Use these to find available frequencies for your wireless equipment anywhere. Equipment operating on a single fixed frequency runs the risk of interference from the strong signals from a local radio or TV station, so it's important to be able to adjust your equipment to an unused channel.

### Recordings

Do you have recordings to play as part of your presentation? A short burst of music; a brief quote from an authority; perhaps an extract from a speech? Any of these can find a place, and if so, it has to be clear. There's no benefit in giving your audience sound with hiss, noise, or distortion.

So start at the beginning. Make sure your source material is as good a quality as you can get. As with any of these aids, seek out those who have skills in areas where you don't.

### Playback Options

With .mp3 and .wav files this is easy. But you might still be using other media, or may have to. Your audio could be fed into a computer, converted to MP3 format, and downloaded into an MP3 player. There you can title the track for identification, and arrange the order. Apple's iPads and iPhones are perhaps the best on the market, and allow you to use .wav or .aiff audio files for better quality than MP3. They also have a high-quality audio output whose level you can adjust on the machine. On any of these small battery-powered items, including your phone, beware the auto shutdown after a short time of inactivity. If your sound snippets are widely separated, you'll have to deal with the delay in restarting the equipment. It's manageable, but you have to do the managing.

If you are a well-organized individual, maybe you can deliver your presentation and play the audio yourself, but it's better to have an assistant with a well-written cue sheet and clearly labeled or titled material.

### Equipment

Unless your group is very small — i.e., can fit around a table — don't rely on the speakers in your laptop, tablet or phone. They aren't up to the task. Some external arrangement of amplifier and speaker is required. If you're really desperate, you might try placing a mike against the laptop speakers and using the house PA to do the work, but this is no more than an emergency situation.

A portable "boombox" might be enough for a small group. If so, it can usually play either cassettes or CDs with ease. Some will have a spare input that you can use to feed in from an MP3 player, so that you're using the boombox for its amplifier and speakers only. For a small room, a useful alternative is to send audio via cable or Bluetooth to a small but powerful Bluetooth speaker such as the Bose Soundlink or Soundlink Mini.

Be careful to place it high, so that the sound reaches over the heads to the back. If you just place it on the table beside you, the front few rows will absorb most of the sound, and those at the back will hear little.

Better sound equipment shouldn't be a problem in a college, or a hotel or conference center. Most will have a sound system available for you to use. There may even be a selection of audio cables to help connect your audio device to their system. If there isn't a technician available to help, you may need a knowledgeable friend or assistant.

*Figure 63. Bose Soundlink Mini*

## AUDIO HORROR STORY

The speaker was introduced, rose, and placed a sheaf of notes on the lectern. We heard loud riffling noises as the pages were arranged. The presenter blew into the microphone, causing an amplified and distorted roar that made everyone wince, and then tapped it for good measure. A few throat clearings, and the presenter launched into the opening remarks, but swayed from side to side, producing loud blasts interspersed with quieter spells. With luck, we heard up to half of what was said.

PRESENTATION PURPOSE
— to engage and inform audience

THE PROBLEM
— poor mike technique

RESULT
— audience minimally engaged, partly informed

SOLUTIONS
— let the PA system do its job
— stay within range of the mike

## 6.4 PRESENTER'S VIEW (OR DISPLAY)

PowerPoint and Keynote allow you to see the slides in a couple of important ways as you edit and assemble your deck of images. Sometimes I see a presentation in which the presenter simply runs through the slides in "navigator" view. This means the slide is shown smaller than it would be if the presentation is in "play," and it also means that the viewer sees all the extraneous menus of the software. If that isn't showing your underware, I don't know what is. I can think of no good reason to ever do that. Play your presentation so that the viewer sees only the images, and not the distractions. Remember also that when you're sharing your screen (in Zoom or similar) other participants will also see the split screen.

Both Keynote and PowerPoint offer a presenter's view. This lets the audience see what you intend them to see, while you, the presenter, see more. The presenter's view is what you see in a rehearsal: to see it while presenting it has to be enabled or selected. PowerPoint allows you a wider range of options than Keynote, but the most important feature is that both allow you to see both the current slide that the audience sees, and the next. That means you aren't taken by surprise as you go from one slide to the next. Make sure you don't spend too much time checking the next slide. You risk paying less attention to your audience.

This example is from a presentation on the history of golf.

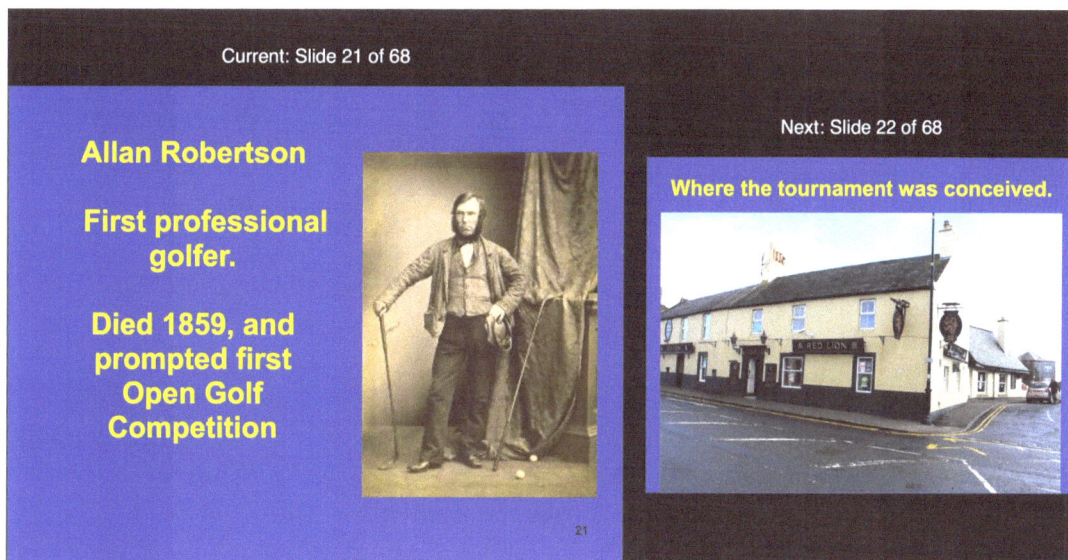

*Figure 64. Presenter's View*

The presenter's view shows the slide the audience sees (the left image) and the next image (on the right). If the current slide has animations, the view shows the current slide, and the current slide with the next stage of animation.

Each image can be moved and resized. The real time clock can be selected, as can a timer showing either elapsed time since the start of the presentation, or remaining time.

As an Apple user, I often use an iPad as a remote control for a Keynote presentation on a laptop. This is easy to set up if the venue has WiFi available, since both devices have to be on the same network. With the iPad mounted on a mike stand, it's easy to see, and a tap on any part of the screen activates the slide change. If I happen to be beside the laptop, I can still change slides there, and the presenter's view on the iPad is updated.

An iPhone can also be used in this way, but the smaller screen means I am tempted to carry it in order to see it properly, and doing so increases the risk of accidentally touching the screen and having a mistimed slide change. For me, the iPad (or iPhone) on a stand is a safer bet.

If there are presenter notes to any or all of the slides, they can be included in the presenter's view. They show in an area along the lower part of my presenter's view where they can be read. I'm not keen on doing this except for rehearsals, since it takes my eyes away from the audience. It's all too easy to find yourself looking only at the laptop screen. As indicated elsewhere, I prefer to use a planner with headings.

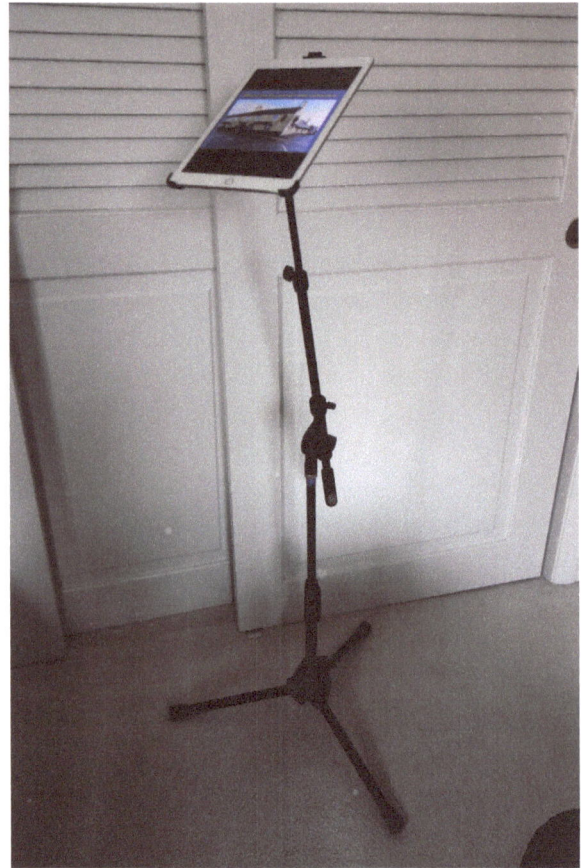

*Figure 65. iPad on stand*

### Autoplay and Looping

PowerPoint and Keynote presentations can be set to start automatically when opened, run from start to finish, and loop from the end back to the beginning. This allows a presentation to run continuously at a conference or exhibition booth, hotel foyer, etc.

First you have to decide if this presentation should run with or without audio.

If audio is to be included, you can run the presentation using the laptop's built-in mike, or with a microphone plugged in, and record your commentary — it's an option under the "Play" heading. Playback is usually through a TV which takes care of the sound. A setting in the laptop may have to be changed to send the audio to the TV instead of to the internal speakers.

If the playback is through a digital projector, many have built-in speakers, but better audio quality is available using an external amplifier and speaker. Refer back to Section 6.3.

A silent presentation needs careful planning, and possibly more text. The timing will have to be arranged so that people have time to read the text and view the images. Display can be on a suitable monitor, TV or projector.

A presentation can also be converted to movie format if required, with or without audio.

The movie version is useful if you want to have your presentation on YouTube, Facebook, or any other video platform, or send it by email. Movie files may be too large to send on some email systems, but can be shared in the cloud (e.g., iCloud, Dropbox, etc.). It may sometimes be more convenient to mail it on a DVD or to show it using a DVD player.

## 6.5 WORDS ALONE MAY NOT BE ENOUGH

**Pictures, they say, are worth a thousand words, and any presentation can be enhanced by the appropriate use of some visual aids. Here are some options.**

### Flip Charts

The flip chart is a large pad of blank paper, usually 80 sheets of A2 size. Each page is serrated near the top so that it can be easily torn out, and some are of the "Post-it" type, with a glue strip near the top so they can be torn out and stuck to a wall or to furniture. The latter are useful for workshops, but they cost a little more and are not normally necessary for presentations.

### Flip Chart Pros and Cons

| Pro | Con |
|---|---|
| Relatively inexpensive | Small size – best with groups up to 30 or so |
| Widely available | Clarity depends on your handwriting technique |
| Stands and charts transportable – lightweight | Stands and charts are an awkward shape for carrying |
| No power required | You have to turn your back to the audience to write |
| Pages can be prepared beforehand, at short notice if necessary. | Best restricted to bold colors, usually red, green, black, blue |
| Visible in normal lighting | Not normally printable |
| Can be stored for future use | Vulnerable to wear and tear |
| Sequence can be changed easily | Turning the pages over can be distracting |

*TABLE 7*

### 35mm Slide Projector

There are good reasons why this format endures. Color slides give excellent results and were once very popular. Many survive, and not everyone has the time or resources to digitize large slide collections. Slides have been known to collect a little condensation in cold conditions, so make sure any slides you use are brought to the venue and aired well before presentation time.

Slide projectors usually require a dark or semi dark room, and the lens usually needs the projector to be well back in the room.

You have three options.

1.  Use a remote control so that you can speak from beside the screen.
2.  Operate the projector by hand, standing beside or behind it. In a small venue this might work, and in a larger one you might need a wireless mike or a mike on a long enough cord to reach you. You'll be strongly tempted to stand facing the screen instead of the audience.
3.  Use an assistant who can work to a script and change the slides on cue. Try to avoid the repetitive 'next slide please' unless you want to lull your audience to sleep.

The danger of remote or assisted operation is loss of sequence. To avoid having to constantly turn round to see which slide is there, use a small mirror that you can set on your lectern or table so that you can see the screen. You know your material well enough that you'll be able to recognize them this way. I've used a small mirror from a toilet bag, and fixed it in place with a lump of Blu Tack.

Should you need to point to something on the screen, the same material can be used to steady your laser pointer (you wouldn't dream of standing in front of the screen to point to something, would you?) and avoid the demented bee syndrome.

## 35MM SLIDES HORROR STORY

A presentation on early mountaineering exploits had drawn a substantial and interested crowd. It was a chilly winter's night, but inside we were enthralled by the earlier part of the presentation, which focused on the planning and preparations for an expedition. The slideshow began, and as the first dozen or so slides came into view, little droplets of condensation evaporated in the heat of the projector, creating intriguing little patterns. The presenter had his slides in glass mounts for protection, but had forgotten that the glass is prone to condensation, and hadn't given them time to warm up beforehand.

PRESENTATION PURPOSE
– to engage audience and encourage donations

THE PROBLEM
– poor use of aids

RESULT
– audience engagement reduced, donations less than anticipated

SOLUTIONS
– experience and improved preparation

### Digital Projector

More and more presentations involve the combination of a laptop and a projector, mainly using Keynote or PowerPoint. This makes for a versatile presentation system, but also leads to the fundamental piece of bad practice which gives this book its subtitle. How often have you sat waiting for the start of a presentation, only to be entertained and diverted by the sight of the presenter's desktop and the series of folders and files being clicked through? (*This is classic 'showing your underware!'*). At any cinema, you expect to see nothing until the title comes up, and so it should be with a presentation. The projector has to be switched on and warmed up, but it's easy to put something in front of the lens to block the image until you are ready to start. Some projectors even include a small cover which can be slid over for this purpose, but this isn't much use on ceiling-mounted projectors. See Section 6.12.

### Video

Your presentation may call for one or more video extracts. By far the best way to do this is to drop them into a PowerPoint or Keynote slide where they can play either automatically, or on click. Another technique is to use iMovie or similar and play it through your laptop or tablet and a data projector. The audio may be carried by HDMI, or you can take it from the headphone socket into a boombox, or PA system. Remember to tell the laptop where to send the sound, or you risk silence.

### Television

An increasing number of venues use modern television. These are usually wall mounted, sometimes on a swivel mount. Any of these large-screen TV sets should have sufficiently high resolution to take an HDMI signal from the laptop. Make sure you present from a position that doesn't block the view of the screen, and check your progress on your laptop screen so that you don't have to turn round to check the TV screen.

For TV, the right connecting cables and/or adaptors are essential. For example, modern MacBooks (Air or Pro) have USB C outputs, and a small adaptor is needed to convert that to HDMI output. Again, remember to tell your laptop where to send the sound.

## 6.6 ADDING AUDIO

**In many presentations, you may want to add an audio or video track. This isn't particularly difficult to do, but you'll want to do it well, and that takes a little more effort.**

The first technique is in some ways the easiest. If you have your audio files in iTunes or similar, you can import them into PowerPoint or Keynote, and play them as part of a slide.

To play your presentation on a different computer or device from the one you used to create the presentation, choose Keynote > Preferences (from the Keynote menu at the top of your screen), click General at the top of the preferences window, then select "Copy audio and movies into document." Doing so ensures the soundtrack is available whenever you play the presentation.

### Laptop

There is a range of software available to help you organize and manage audio and video. Both PowerPoint and Keynote will accept audio and video files, so you can integrate them into your presentation. Most laptops now have music-playing software, and there is a range of video players available, so for a single audio or video file, you might consider these. Most laptops and tablets have a good quality headphone output that can be connected directly to some sort of sound system (see laptop sound below).

Whatever the source of your original material (CD, radio, etc.) you can create audio files and store them in an appropriately named folder. iTunes is particularly well suited to this. Create a playlist and add the tracks you need. Call up the playlist and you can use them in any order you choose, adjust sound levels directly and even apply different equalization on the fly.

### Laptop Sound

Modern laptops come equipped with remarkably good little speakers — but don't expect to use them for a presentation if the audience is bigger than four or five. For small groups you need a small external speaker system, and there are several on the market. Below are some characteristics to look for. It helps to be prepared with a set of connectors to enable you to connect to a house system. Since the laptop sound is almost certainly a 3.5mm jack output, you need a 3.5mm jack to XLR male, and a 3.5mm jack to 6mm (quarter inch) jack plug as a basic minimum. That will be sufficient for the majority of situations. A well-organized conference venue will probably have the relevant connectors, but smaller venues are less likely to, as mentioned below.

### USB Powered

Convenient, but limits the power and volume available. A battery powered system will usually be louder and better.

### Bluetooth Speaker

The market now offers a number of Bluetooth speakers (see figure 63), and some of them quite powerful. They can be placed anywhere, since there are no cables to connect. Just make sure the built-in battery is fully charged before you start.

### Powered Speaker

A single box with the amplifier and speakers built in is convenient and easier to use. The stereo effect will be minimal even with a small group so even a single speaker will work well.

Separate speakers mean more cable to lay out and pack away and unless stereo sound is essential to the presentation the inconvenience probably isn't worth it.

### Speaker Orientation

Check how the system stands. Some speakers that are sold for computer use either clip to a monitor or stand beside it. Often, they are tilted up to project sound from where they sit on the desk toward your ears. The problem is that if you position these speakers beside your laptop, the sound is absorbed by the front row of your group and those at the back can't hear much. Square shapes are easier to pack and to work with. Have you ever tried to tie a rounded speaker to anything?

### Cable Length

Get a couple of connecting cables. A short one of two to three meters (six to nine feet) will do for very small groups, and at least double that for larger groups. Why? With a smaller group putting the speaker(s) beside the laptop might be sufficient, but with a bigger group you need to get the speaker(s) higher to project over the front row and reach the folks at the back. For a short presentation I've even stood and held a speaker in my hand. The longer cable gives you more reach to the tops of bookcases or other furniture. I have a small JBL system which is light enough to be tied to a mike stand but loud enough to fill the average meeting room or classroom.

### Battery or AC Powered

I'd go for battery every time because of laziness. Less cable to lay out, involves no wall wart power supplies, fewer power outlets to find and less trouble all round. I have on occasion used a small guitar practice amplifier, which gave good results but was a lot more to carry. Fresh (or freshly charged) batteries every time is the rule. Otherwise you court disaster.

For larger groups and conferences, the laptop has to tie into the venue's sound system. You can make life a lot easier (and win friends with sound engineers) if you carry a cable that fits your laptop headphone socket at one end and has an XLR male connector at the other. That XLR connection means your laptop is just like a mike and will fit into all but the most basic sound systems.

I once turned up at a conference with such a cable and it was the only one there. I handed it over, and the sound engineer was spared both censure for not having one, and the urgent need to create one, so I got special attention. Another way to ensure the admiration of the sound engineer is to do a level check with your laptop and then promise not to adjust the sound level on the laptop before presentation time. Leave any adjustment to the sound engineer. That person knows the house acoustics, knows how much sound an audience will "soak up" and how much to turn up the gain to compensate. Any adjustment you make will be less than helpful.

Should you find yourself presenting at a major conference, you might have the opportunity to work with a teleprompter. These were originally developed for television newsreaders, and are now widely used by politicians making speeches. You're unlikely to see any major political figure make a significant speech without one.

Like anything else, the teleprompter has its pros and cons. For set speeches, it works well. The text is usually released in advance (and embargoed until delivery so that the press can't use it until then) and the politician sticks to the carefully constructed script. For you, that's the downside. A teleprompter shows you the text of your speech, and you deviate from that at your peril.

In a professional teleprompter, the text is transferred to a computer that projects the text at a legible size in a rolling display which is matched to your speaking speed. The image is projected onto an angled piece of glass placed at a comfortable height for you to see. You can read it, but all the audience sees is a piece of glass. At a major venue, there are usually two, one on each side, so you can look from one to the other and appear to be scanning the audience.

A cheaper version is to use a teleprompter app on your tablet, which has to be carefully placed so that you can see it clearly. It helps if you are doing the same speech several times, or have time to do several rehearsals, and if you lose your place, it's difficult to get back on track.

It takes some getting used to, partly because you see only a small section of text at a time, and partly because you also have to adjust the pace at which it appears. Practice before you do your first teleprompter presentation, but my suggestion is to use it only for short speeches, not for presentations. It demands too much of your attention and diverts you from other aspects of your presentation, such as listening to your audience.

## 6.7 USING FLIP CHARTS

**Old technology but simple, reliable, cheap and versatile**
**Ideal for small groups, workshops, etc.**
**Surprisingly effective when used properly**
**Particularly useful for developing ideas or recording discussion points**

### Using the Flip Chart

If a flip chart is part of your presentation, first check that there are enough pages left on the pad. Whatever number of pages you think you'll need, if the pad has less than twice that number left, bring along another pad just in case. Even if the venue promises that they have one, I always have a spare pad in the car, or have checked out where I can get one locally. If you read between the lines, you can tell that I was once caught out that way.

Next, consider the stand or easel. Writing on a flip chart requires a stable easel with a firm backing for the pad such as the one illustrated below (Figure 66). Four legged models are even more stable (Figure 60), usually at the expense of weight.

*Figure 66. Flipchart Stand 1*

*Figure 67. Flipchart Stand 2*

**Being Practical**

I use an easel like the one on the right (Figure 67) for portability. It holds the pad on the bar at the top, but gives no support for writing on the pad, so I use it as an announcement board at the entrance to a room, or at one side. In that case, I place the pad on a table to write the announcement before attaching it to the easel.

Make sure your flip chart is positioned so that everyone can see it. Walk around the room to check, allowing for heads to be in the way. If you can leave the stand in position then do so, but you may have to mark its position if that space is needed for some other purpose beforehand. A couple of small pieces of sticky tape are enough to do the job, and are easily removable afterwards without damaging the floor surface.

You need to stand to one side so that people can see the chart, but you need to turn the pages, and you may also need to point to key words or diagrams. A laser pointer can be used, but with care (see 6.11 – Laser Pointer Guidelines).

Never direct a laser pointer toward the audience, or anyone else. A good alternative is a short piece of dowel, available from almost any hardware store. Paint it black, and color each end of it to make it visible. An alternative to paint is to use some yellow tape. The dowel needs to be only a little longer than the page is wide — at least 24 inches or 60 centimeters. That's long enough to be useful, short enough to be portable.

Instead of a dowel, try quarter round, which has two flat sides. It won't roll away from you, and the flat side makes it easier to stick things to it. I once saw a presenter who glued a Santa from a Christmas card to the end of her quarter-round pointer for a mid-December presentation. Instead of just pointing to her page, this ploy allowed her to say, "Now let's see what Santa thinks is important here." It certainly made the event more memorable.

One advantage of flip charts is that you can easily go back to a previous page, for example if there's a question. To make it easy, use little Post-it notes as tabs to identify each page, creating a flip chart index. Place them on the side of each page in turn, and write a title on the exposed part of the tab. At the end, bring all your pages to the front, and it's easy to read the tabs, and find a specific page.

For this reason, I've seen people use the flip chart in reverse. Most users start with the flip chart pad on the stand, and pull the pages up out of the way in turn as they go through the presentation. At the end, with the last page on view, all the others are hanging over the back of the stand. Some prefer to start that way, and pull the pages down in sequence, ending with the entire pad on the stand. It's a matter of personal preference. I prefer the first way, for one reason only. It means I start with all the tabs in view, and it makes it easier to skip a page if I need to. The other way makes that option a little more difficult.

Preparing a flip chart is important. Writing on it doesn't need to be a chore. The advantage is that you are going to write large, and the audience is going to see it smaller. If you are going to write freehand on anything, this is it. Avoid the temptation to select any old marker pen. Many, especially permanent markers, will bleed through from one sheet to the next. It's worth searching around for pens designed to be used on flip charts.

Chisel point pens allow you to write using thick lines, which should be easily visible, but there is another way that you might consider. On your computer you probably have lettering style options that include "outline." Have a look if you're not sure how that looks. Outline lettering can be fairly easy to draw, and very effective for the audience (see 9.1). You can draw the letters with rounded corners if you prefer.

Other tricks with flip charts include reveals and additions. A reveal is easy enough. You might have two diagrams on one page. You want the audience to see both, but you want to discuss one and then show the other. Simply tack a blank page over it with a tiny amount of sticky tape — enough to hold the page in place, but not so much that you can't remove it easily. Practice beforehand to work out how much you need.

If you're asking the audience to come up with a set of words or ideas, and you know what to expect from them, you can prepare a page with the words already there, and cover each with a small piece of paper. Write the word lightly on the paper with a pencil so that you can see it, but they can't. As the words come from the audience, pull the paper off to reveal it on your flip chart page. Seeing pieces of paper covering up the remaining words is usually an incentive, and if appropriate, you could arrange them in alphabetical order as an added clue.

Additions are also easy. One technique I saw used Post-it notes on which the presenter had drawn colored stars and arrows, and cut around the outlines. He placed these here and there to emphasize specific points. It is cheap, effective, and removable afterwards so that you can use the pages again.

The situation may call for things to be written up on the page. This is more likely in a workshop than a presentation, but you may need to do it. For example, you could invite the audience to provide you with dates, names or numbers.

First, use a separate flip chart, on your other side. The audience attention moves to that side for the exercise, and then you bring them back to your main presentation. This also allows you to use your main pad to show the question, and leaves the data in view while you move on to any other pages that require it. Remember to cover the data when you have finished.

Second, have somebody else do the writing. An assistant who can walk on and write the information as it comes in allows you to keep contact with the audience rather than turning your back to them as you write.

Should you need to draw something during the presentation, there's an easy way to make sure you get it right first time. Draw it beforehand in light pencil. The audience won't be able to see this 'ghost image' from where they sit, but you will, and following the lines means your drawing will take shape quickly and accurately. I've also seen some presenters who drew light pencil lines on the page to help them keep their writing straight, and it's fairly common to draw the axes for a graph in pen, but pencil in the shape of the curve for completion during the presentation.

Flip Chart pages also available in 'Post-it' format. The ability to remove a page from the pad and stick it to the wall is often very useful in workshops, but please first check that the wall surface is suitable.

| Availability | Widely available and fairly cheap. |
|---|---|
| Portability | Good – the charts and stands may be an awkward shape, but are light enough to be carried quite easily. |
| Power needs | None. |
| Positioning | Needs to be to your side so that you can reach it. |
| Height | Adjustable for comfortable writing. |
| Visibility | If you are on the same floor level as the audience, raise it as high as it will go.<br><br>If you are on a higher level, place it a comfortable height for you.<br><br>Clearly visible in normal lighting if you use it properly.<br><br>Obscured as you turn to write on it. |
| Versatility | Handles text and graphics – limitation is that nearly everything has to be hand drawn.<br><br>Easy to go back to any point in the sequence. |

*TABLE 8*


## 6.8 USING OVERHEAD PROJECTORS

**Still very useful when working with small groups**
**Especially useful for interactive workshops**
**Some venues are likely to still have an OHP as part of their standard equipment**

OHPs were once the workhorse of presentations. They are still widely available, simple to operate, and excellent for small group presentations and workshops. It might be worthwhile investing in your own if you feel the demand will justify it, in which case you'll probably want one of the portable models that fold neatly into a carry case. More usually you'll be using one at the venue, and it really is important to check it out beforehand. Especially important is making sure that the bulb works, and that a spare is available if needed. Also check for dust on the lens and on the light table. Clean both if necessary.

## OHP Operation

Position is the first hurdle. The projector has to be placed to throw a large enough image on the screen, but conveniently near to you so that you can operate it. Ideally, the screen will be of the type that allows you to tilt out the top edge so that it slopes down to the back. A vertical screen is likely to give you what is called a 'keystone' image — wider at the top than at the bottom. A small amount is acceptable, but it distorts the image and is best avoided. If the screen is vertical, the projection head has to be at the height of the middle of the screen to avoid keystoning, i.e., the image is wider at the top. This is unlikely unless the screen is floor mounted, which probably places it too low for everyone to see. A tilted screen means it can be higher than the projector, so the audience has a clearer line of sight.

The projector has to be square on to the center of the screen. For a screen on the back wall, this means it takes center stage, and you have to be slightly to the side. If the screen is in the corner, this still applies. Are you left or right-handed? If you're right-handed you should position the projector to your right as you face the audience, especially if you intend to write on any of the transparencies.

Switching on is usually straightforward. A switch is commonly on top or on the front. Some use a large bar, others a more conventionally shaped switch. Just be sure you know where the switch is before you stand up to talk.

Some models also have a normal/bright switch. As the names suggest, normal is enough for a normally lit room, and the bright setting helps in a brighter room, or if you have to throw the light farther to get a larger than usual image. Some will also have a lamp change switch. These models have two bulbs, and if one dies, you turn the switch to bring the other into use. If you find one of these projectors, always check that two bulbs are fitted, and that both are working.

The projector's lens head will usually tilt up and down to raise or lower the image, so that you can adjust it for minimum keystoning. On some, a mirror is tilted, on others the whole head will swivel.

Focusing is simple, once you have worked out which knob to turn. Essentially the focus operates by raising or lowering the arm on which the projector head is mounted. Some have a fixed vertical arm, usually in the right rear corner, and the projector head moves up and down the arm, so the focus knob is where the two arms meet. Others have a one-piece arm, and the focus knob is where the arm is fastened to the main body of the machine. A simple technique is to place a pencil or pen on the projector table, and switch on. Focus to get a sharp edge, and that's it.

The focus check also allows you to see if the machine is clean. Dust and other material can affect an OHP, and most of it is easy to clean. First the light table — the top of the machine where you'll be placing your transparencies. A wipe with a moist tissue (such as 'Wet Ones'), followed by a dry tissue or cloth will usually be enough. Next the projection head, which has a lens where the light comes in from the light table, and a lens where the light leaves, heading for the screen. Both of these areas can attract dust, and the same cleaning technique applies.

If dust is still a problem, and especially if it's around the edges of the screen, you need to go inside (or get someone to do it for you). Unless it's a portable, light from the lamp comes up through a special lens that is protected by a plain sheet of glass. This glass sheet is the light table that we've already cleaned, but dust can get into the machine and lie on this lens which is visible as a series of concentric grooves under the glass. On most machines the glass sheet is held in place by strips of metal that are screwed to the top of the machine. After you have disconnected the power cord, undo these, lift the glass, and clean the lens as before.

Do the underside of the glass sheet while you're at it. A resident technician can do this for you, but it's best to know how to do it for yourself, because as we all know, the very time you need this done will be the time when there is no technician, and nobody else has a clue about it.

### OHP Aids

There are a couple of things that can help you get the best out of your OHP presentation.

The first is a pointer. The last thing you want to do is walk to the screen and point to it. You've lost eye contact with the audience, and you're blinded by the projector. For some of the audience, you've become part of the screen, and of the image projected onto it. For others, you are casting a large shadow on the screen. Definitely a no-no. But you need to point to a particular bar on a bar graph, or a particular year, or something. You need a pointer that you can lay on the light table.

A pencil is good. It casts a clear image on the screen, and already has a point. Use a hexagonal one rather than a round one, so it won't roll off the table. An extra-long cocktail stick is another option, but it tends to roll away, and once I used an ordinary drinking straw, with a blob of Blu Tack on the end. The Blu Tack was shaped like a small arrowhead, and its weight helped to keep the straw in place. Another effective ploy was an arrow shape cut out of the back of a cereal box.

The second is a reveal sheet. It's not something to use often, but there can be times when you want the audience to see the top part of a slide, and then the rest. The simplest way to do this is to place a page on the light table to hide the relevant part. The problem is that the page will tend to slide away, so you need something to hold it in place. One answer is Blu Tack again. A couple of small blobs will allow you to stick the page in place. It'll stay there until you need to remove it, and will come away easily. Another is to tape a couple of heavy objects to the top corners of the page. US coins are too lightweight for this, but the UK's one pound coin is small and heavy — ideal. If you don't feel like risking the cash, rummage around in a workshop for a couple of heavy washers which will do nicely instead. With the weight in place, the page will stay where you place it.

### OHP Technique

An important strength of the overhead projector is that you can retain eye contact with and voice projection to the audience, and yet so many presenters throw that away by standing up at the screen to point, or by turning round to look at the screen as they talk. Neither is good practice. If you have the machine set up properly, you know what they are seeing, and all you need to do to check is briefly drop your gaze to the light table.

Try using mounts or holders for your slides. A slide on a light table on its own looks amateurish and there are large edge areas which distract. Mounts are simple card frames to which the transparency can be taped. They are cheap and easy to use, and you can write titles and notes on the mount to help you.

Cardboard holders are more expensive, but offer far better protection to transparencies that you might use frequently. They can be held in a ring binder for storage, and you can write titles on the holder so that you can find the ones you need for a particular occasion.

Changing the slides is important. Sounds easy — just slide one off and lay down another? No. This treats your audience to the distraction of one large image sliding away, a large empty screen, and then another slide maneuvering into position. Each slide has a shelf life. When it has served its purpose, switch off the machine and change to the next slide. When it's time, switch on and there it is. Alternatively, cover the slide with a page (creating a dark screen), remove the old slide, insert the new one under the page, and remove the page.

Doing this has two benefits. First, you deny the audience the distraction of the slide change. Second, you refocus their attention on you until it's time to look at another slide.

### OHP Slides

Simple, easy-to-read slides are essential. These days it is so easy to prepare good OHP slides that there is little excuse for bad ones.

First, what should you use?

### Transparencies

OHP transparencies come in two main categories — write-on and printable. Transparencies for writing on range from thin and flimsy to thick and robust. Thinner is cheaper, but thicker is far better.

### Pens

Avoid the temptation to select any old marker pen. Many just won't work on OHP sheets. The transparencies are designed to hold the ink from a pen, and the right pens are designed to give a heavier than normal ink flow. The choice can seem daunting, but is really fairly simple. If you plan to write your own transparencies, you need the right pens for the job.

Water based or waterproof. There's little doubt here. A classroom teacher who might be using OHPs on a daily basis and using the same slide several times will probably use waterproof (or 'permanent') pens for the basic slide, and add notes with a water-based pen. This means the notes can be wiped off with a moist cloth and the slide reused. If you plan to use any slides this way, you should do the same. Otherwise use water-based pens. On screen, you can't tell the difference, but the water-based pens allow you to correct errors, and to reuse transparencies.

Points. You'll find a range of pen styles — fine and medium points, round or chisel. Forget fine. The lines are too thin to be seen, and the very least that you should you use is medium point. Even then, unless your group is very small, you'll find that you can't just write on the transparency as you would on a page. You'll need a technique or two aimed at improving the visibility of what you write, such as those on the next few pages.

I prefer the heavier point, and chisel style, but round can be as effective. I've seen some excellent handwritten transparencies, and the authors were nearly always artists or calligraphers who were able to craft the information on to the transparency with clarity and style. Most of us can't aspire to this, and the printed transparency is our best hope.

Printable transparencies are available for inkjet and laser printers, and for Xerox style copiers. It's important to get the right transparencies for your printer or copier, and although the manufacturer will probably sell you a version, I've found the generic ones from the big retail and office supply houses to be just as good.

On balance it's probably better to print your transparencies directly from your computer. Copiers will do a good job, but the clarity is not always quite as good. However the difference is not so great that we need to worry about it, and cost or convenience may be the determining factor.

### OHP Transparency Design
*(N.B. – These principles also apply to PowerPoint/Keynote presentations)*

**Whether you're hand writing or printing, Clear, Big and Bold are the words to remember.**

Use large fonts and abide by the Rule of Seven. It's simple. No more than seven lines per slide, or seven words per line. For overhead slides, around 24-point fonts are a good choice for the main text; headings should be larger.

Newspaper headlines are a good indicator of what to do. They are invariably a sans serif typeface, and you can usually read them some distance away.

If you are using transparencies, you might want to use "portrait" orientation; that is, with the long dimension running vertically. (35 mm slides are usually used in "landscape" orientation.)

Most of the audience will not be able to see the bottom of the screen, so put things in the top two-thirds of the slide, and leave the bottom blank (except for page numbers). Always number your slides, in case they get out of order. Use the slide mount for this purpose.

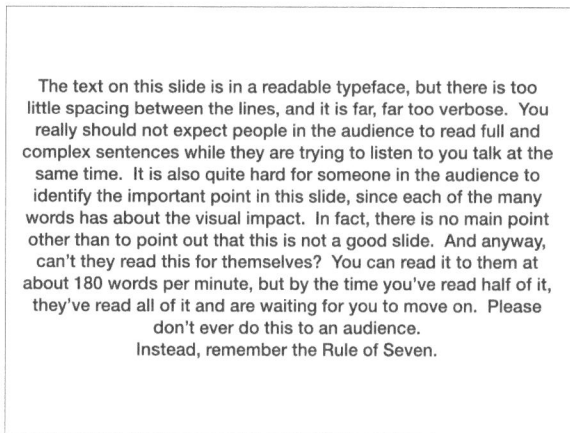

The text on this slide is in a readable typeface, but there is too little spacing between the lines, and it is far, far too verbose. You really should not expect people in the audience to read full and complex sentences while they are trying to listen to you talk at the same time. It is also quite hard for someone in the audience to identify the important point in this slide, since each of the many words has about the visual impact. In fact, there is no main point other than to point out that this is not a good slide. And anyway, can't they read this for themselves? You can read it to them at about 180 words per minute, but by the time you've read half of it, they've read all of it and are waiting for you to move on. Please don't ever do this to an audience.
Instead, remember the Rule of Seven.

*Figure 68. Not good*

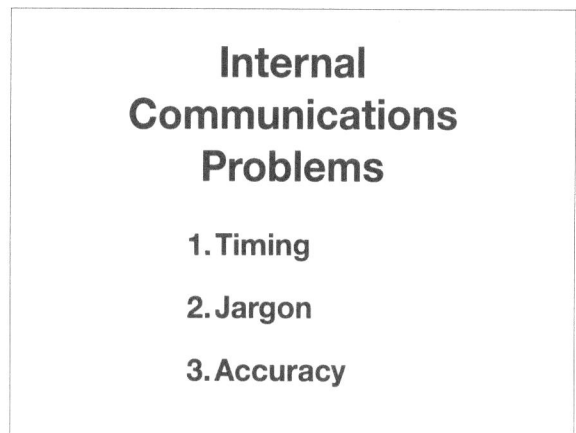

# Internal Communications Problems

1. Timing

2. Jargon

3. Accuracy

*Figure 69. Better slide*

Figure 68 is not a good slide — far too much text! Figure 69 is simple — clearly visible — and allows the presenter to develop each point in turn.

If you use overhead transparencies in "landscape" orientation, make sure that your text does not run past the horizontal margin of a standard overhead projector.

If your slides include diagrams, use fat lines and large fonts. Thin lines are hard to see.

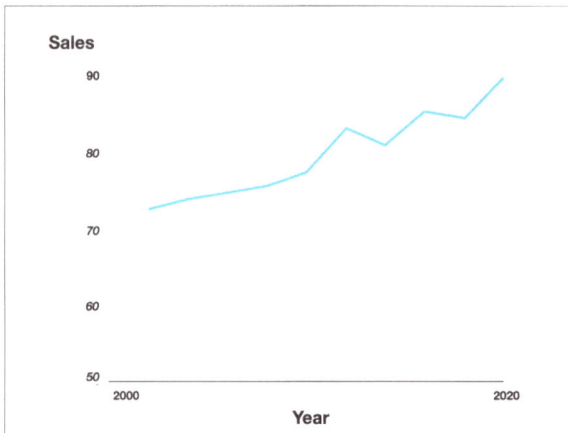

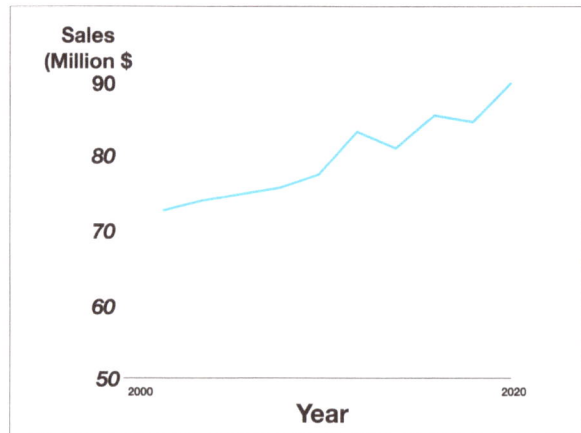

In Figure 70, the curve in the graph will show up well, but the axis labels are too small.

Figure 71 will show up better on the screen. The axis labels are larger and clearer, and the vertical scale has been tidied.

You might have graphs showing how some quantity varies as a function of some other quantity. Make sure the curves use fat lines; if you have multiple curves on one graph, either use obviously distinctive line styles, or (perhaps better) clearly contrasting colors. Label the axes with large fonts, including complete scale information. Be honest: don't play games with the scale or origin to make your curves look better than they really are.

Color is helpful, if used with care. You can't go far wrong with bold primary colors. Pastels may be more subtle, but they just don't work as well. Use two or three colors in the text of your slides, and use it consistently. You can use color in diagrams to categorize graphical elements. In graphs with several curves, you'll find that contrasting colors for each line are more effective than different line styles.

## OHP HORROR STORY

The speaker is introduced, walks to the overhead projector and searches around to find the switch. The screen is brightly lit and you look at it, wondering what is to come. After a few moments a slide swims into view, jerks this way and that until it is properly in place, and then comes into focus. It is a copy of a typed page, and you wish you had taken that front row seat after all, so that you might manage to read it. The presenter waves in its general direction, making some point, and then the slide is whisked away, leaving that brightly lit screen to entertain you for the next few minutes.

PRESENTATION PURPOSE
– to engage and inform audience

PROBLEMS
– unfamiliarity with the equipment
– poor OHP technique
– failure to obey Rule of Seven

RESULT
– audience less engaged and less informed

SOLUTIONS
– practice with equipment
– learn good technique
– learn Rule of Seven

## 6.9 CREATING HANDOUTS

**Handouts are easy to produce and can help your audience to remember your presentation, and you.**

The decision on handouts depends on such things as cost, audience size, etc., but let's think about why you might want to use them.

- ✓ While showing slides with simple, easy-to-understand graphs and data, you might want your audience to have more detail
- ✓ There might be maps or technical drawings and diagrams that form part of your presentation and which are too complex for a screen
- ✓ A handout can remind the audience of your main points
- ✓ You might want to take the opportunity to make sure that everyone has your contact details
- ✓ It provides the opportunity to include an evaluation page

Assuming you want to involve handouts, what is to be included? The last thing you want to leave people is the straightforward text of your presentation, unless it's the delivery of an academic paper, in which the text is the key element and the presentation is a guide to it. More usually you have to select what to give people, and this selection can be done at the planning stage.

The first and last things are the easy bit. A title page with the main headings of your presentation provides a useful summary for the audience, and if you can make it visually attractive with design or color, so much the better. The final page should include your contact details, so that anyone who wants to ask questions, or invite you to provide another presentation, can find you.

The bit in between is the tricky bit.

How many pages do you think are needed? A telephone book is too much, and a couple of pages is probably too little unless it's a very short presentation. Up to about 10 pages is probably enough unless there are good reasons to go beyond this.

Here are some of the obvious things you need to include:

- ✓ Copies of graphs and charts, maps or diagrams
- ✓ Headings and subheadings
- ✓ Conclusion
- ✓ Recommendations (if appropriate)

For PowerPoint or Keynote users, this is easy — perhaps too easy. PowerPoint offers the facility to print handouts with a variety of layouts. Three per page is popular, since this allows the audience enough space to write notes alongside each slide. This is a convenient and useful facility, but has a drawback or two. It's tempting to think that every graphic you used in the presentation is so important that it also deserves to be in the handout. I'm not sure that is always true. For example, you may have used a cartoon to elaborate or emphasize a point, but the point is already adequately made in a previous slide, and to include it in the handout might be superfluous. Another case might be where you start with a skeletal diagram and add flesh to it in the presentation. Do you give them the skeleton or the finished version?

Keynote allows you to include the stages of a buildup, but neither PowerPoint nor Keynote allow you to select which slides to print other than a range. Sometimes I use screenshots of the relevant slides, and import them to Pages or Word where I can resize them and add any text. Or just print all of them, and select for copying.

## 6.10 ZOOMING

*Modern video conferences are easier to use than ever before*
*Don't be dazzled by the technology — the basic presentation skills still apply*

### Video Conferences

One-way video, two-way audio conferences have been used successfully for some years for formal presentations such as new product introductions or messages from top management. The presentation is made from a central location; members of the audience can ask questions but are not seen. But the real growth in videoconferencing has been in two-way video and audio conferencing.

Many corporations have videoconferencing facilities to allow groups of people in different places to meet, and universities and colleges now routinely deliver lectures to remote students as part of their distance learning provision. Cheaper hardware and software plus a greater availability of broadband connections means that videoconferencing has moved from the esoteric to the routine. With the outbreak of COVID 19 in 2020, the Zoom platform became a household name and a daily tool for many. Alternatives include Microsoft Teams, Cisco Webex Meetings, Skype, and others.

Some people feel comfortable in a video conference almost immediately. Others break out in a cold sweat just thinking about a video conference, as the fear of giving a speech combines with the tension of operating in an unfamiliar environment. Although most of the rules for conducting meetings and making presentations apply equally well to video conferences, the medium makes some accommodation necessary. If a video conference is in your future, here are some tips based on the experiences of veterans in the business.

Make sure the format is appropriate for your purpose. Zoom means you don't have to travel, but it's more impersonal. Even the most enthusiastic say that video conferences can never substitute for face-to-face meetings because you don't know the participants or how they are likely to react. It can be difficult to look at people as they listen, and gauge their reactions and interest levels. Video conferences may also fail because people do not participate fully so any decisions reached may not represent a real consensus.

On the positive side, many believe that people reach good decisions more quickly during a video conference than when they are in a conventional meeting because they come better prepared and are more aware of time constraints. For some participants, the speed with which decisions are made in video conferences carries over to conventional meetings, and so these meetings improve as a result.

### Professionals agree that video conferences work best for problem solving when
- ✓ You know the people or can talk with them on the phone or in person before the conference
- ✓ The discussion points are known in advance
- ✓ There are no "surprises" — there is agreement on the criteria for the decision
- ✓ None of the decision-makers is known to be against what will be proposed
- ✓ Everyone accepts that the problem needs a solution

### Zoom Etiquette
Experienced Zoom users will know to mute themselves during a presentation, but a reminder is always useful. If you are the host you can run down the list and mute people, but the larger the audience, the more time and effort this takes. If you are not the host, they may offer the reminder. It may also be useful to remind people that if they need to comment, the simplest way is to hold down the space bar, wait for the unmute signal, and then comment. Otherwise they might forget to 're mute'.

### Prepare (and stick to) an agenda
Creating a tight agenda is vital in video conferences; other users may be waiting for the facilities and costs of lengthy meetings are prohibitive. Agendas should be circulated in advance and should include an estimate of the time each item should take, the person responsible for each section of the meeting and those items on which action is expected.

### Adapt your movement and use of eyes for the camera

If you're presenting, make sure you aren't in closeup. A head to waist shot, as used by most news readers, will serve you better since it will allow you a little movement while remaining in shot. Use as much energy as you can muster. Gestures and facial expressions that look theatrical in person look normal on a monitor, and normal gestures can look limp or tired. People expect to see movement on camera and are easily bored by a "talking head." It's especially important to use gestures when you first start to speak so that viewers at the other end won't have to depend on seeing lip movements, or the software's indicators to determine who is speaking. Introducing yourself the first time you speak is also helpful. Since people will usually be close up to a small screen, text can be very much smaller.

### Compensate for the lack of direct eye contact

The absence of real eye contact is one of the major disadvantages of videoconferencing because it is isolating and it makes it difficult to "read" the listeners' reactions and adjust to indications of hostility, disinterest, or confusion. You may want to question those at another site frequently about their reactions, and if you cannot see everyone in the group, imagine them looking at you. If the group is small enough, you can ask everyone in turn for a comment or a yes/no. For larger groups, invite them to use the "Q&A" feature so you can answer later.

### Dress for the camera

Although it's no longer necessary to avoid white shirts, it pays to avoid tartans (sometimes known as plaid in the US), loud colors, boldly striped ties, and large jewelry, all of which distract viewers and take their attention away from the business at hand.

### Dress your background

Many video conferences now use your desktop or laptop computer, so you don't have to leave your home or office. Before participating, check to see what the camera will see when you go live. That large picture window behind you is full of distractions. Perhaps there is a window or picture casting reflections which will affect the camera, or perhaps the wall behind you just doesn't make you look good on TV. How often have you been on a Zoom call during COVID, and seen someone's young child wander into the background and do something entirely distracting?

It's easy to do an office-to-office video conference with a colleague first, or perhaps even swap offices so you can really see it from the other side, and make any necessary adjustments before that important conference call.

If you don't have a suitably distraction-free background, modern software can create one for you. Buy a green background cloth. With that behind you, the software can superimpose a background image. You can appear to be on a beach, on the moon, or anywhere in between. Remember to choose something that helps you achieve your presentation purpose.

Many laptops now have a built-in camera mounted above the top edge of the screen. For many purposes this will be adequate. Laptops also come with a built-in microphone, and for many purposes these too will be adequate. If remote presentations are to become a regular feature for you, a separate camera and mike will be worthwhile. You could go for a combined camera and mike, or separate them.

If you will be sharing your screen, regardless of whether it's PowerPoint, Word, video or anything else, make sure you have it ready before screen sharing is activated. Close all other software so you can find and open what you want quickly.

If you haven't spent some time watching YouTube presenters, you might find it worthwhile. Some are very good, and many are not. Check out the backgrounds, the video and audio quality. Video blogging is beyond the scope of this book, but presentation style and technique will always count.

### Use visual aids

Because people remember best what they both see and hear, visual aids help understanding in any presentation. Any teacher knows the old adage: "I hear I forget, I see I remember, I do I understand." In video conferences, charts and graphs can compensate for some of the problems with the medium — shortage of time, boredom with a relatively fixed environment — by condensing complex data to emphasize relationships and by providing visual change. Beware, however, that the equipment at your site may demand production that is different from what you are accustomed to. If you use a dedicated video conference suite, some videoconferencing managers provide very precise guidelines. Check with your professionals before you start making visuals. If you're using Zoom, and aren't the host, make sure the host knows that you will want to share your screen, and that the host knows how to enable this.

Modern video conference software includes the ability to share screens, or send and receive files. Have those ready in a universally available format such as pdf. If this is an in-house presentation, you'll know which formats to use, but if your audience is mixed, it pays to check beforehand that everyone can read .pdf, .xls, and .jpeg.

The same applies to any audio or video files you may wish to send. In some cases the video conference software allows file distribution and sharing. An alternative is to set up a file-sharing system for participants, such as Dropbox, Google Drive, or Microsoft Teams. Place the files in a suitably named folder, and invite participants to share it.

### Handling questions

Presenting via Zoom can be challenging, not least with questions. I find I have to concentrate on the presentation, paying attention to the screen and to my notes, and prefer to have people ask questions at the end. They can use the "chat" function to pose questions, but I don't look at them until I've finished. Whenever possible I enlist the aid of a helper to sift and sort the questions as I speak, and bring them up at the end, but that isn't always possible.

### Be a good listener

Voice-activated systems may pick up a secondary voice, i.e., a participant asking a question. Regular Zoom participants quickly learn to mute themselves except when they wish to speak. To avoid voice clipping, be careful not to interrupt a speaker or talk to another participant at your site while someone else is talking. One at a time works best, and that too is a discipline (and etiquette) that may carry over into conventional meetings.

Don't forget that the camera sees more than a person can.

If you like to doodle, keep caricatures and pithy comments about fellow participants' mental capacity out of range of your camera. In rooms with voice-activated cameras or software that selects the conference site with active sound, remember that an unmuted side conversation can make you and your friend the focus of the camera's unwelcome attentions. You've probably seen this on Zoom, where an unmuted mike can pick up the dog barking, the clatter of dishes, etc., and since Zoom automatically highlights the thumbnail shot that is the source of the loudest audio, everyone can see who is making that extraneous noise.

One last thought. A video conference is like any meeting, except that one member of the group has that single eye. Know what you want from the meeting and be prepared, and you will be less distracted by that one-eyed participant.

## 6.11 LASER POINTER GUIDELINES

**Laser safety is an important issue here, so the three golden rules for laser pointers are**
1. **Never direct a laser pointer toward anyone**
2. **Never direct a laser pointer toward anyone**
3. **Never direct a laser pointer toward anyone**

**Laser Pointer Guidelines**

We've all seen laser pointers in use. They are excellent for drawing audience attention to a specific part of a graphic; for example, to pick out a single face in a group photo, a component in a circuit diagram or a detail in a blueprint. They are often over-used. I once watched the US Department of Energy do a televised presentation with a laser pointer whose little red dot danced about the screen like a demented bee. That was the first difficulty. The second difficulty was that the graphs were overly complicated, with far too much information on them. Simpler graphics would have been more self-explanatory, and might have eliminated the need for the demented bee.

It may sound so obvious, but if you're going to use a laser pointer, you have to turn away from the audience to watch where the dot goes. This loses eye contact, and so you have to do something to re-establish it afterwards.

First, try to avoid showing a series of graphics that require you to use a laser pointer. Does each one require you to aim a red or green dot at something? Arguably, if you need a laser pointer for a graph, it's too complex a graph and it would be better to simplify it. Use the pointer sparingly — not everything needs to be pointed out.

When you do need to use it, you have to find a way of steadying that dot.

Use a blob of Blu Tack or similar, position it on the edge of the table or lectern, and press the pointer onto it. When you need to use the pointer, press the button, turn it as needed, and the Blu Tack will steady it for you. Release the button and the pointer stays put until the next time you need it. Alternatively, lean your elbow on a table or lectern to steady it, and you'll steady your hand so that the red dot of the laser pointer goes where you want it to go, and stays there fairly steadily. Rather than try to keep it perfectly still, which you won't be able to do, move it slowly

**Being Practical**

and deliberately in a pattern that will allow people to see precisely what you are pointing at. The rapid circling or up and down motion that you may have seen is generally distracting, and less effective. Whatever you do with the pointer requires your attention to be on the image, and that is the biggest reason for being sparing in its use.

After using the pointer, you have to turn back to your audience, and re-establish eye contact. In planning your presentation, identify any place where you'll use the laser pointer, and build in a re-entry device to get you back on track. A simple remark can be enough.

"He looks so much more dignified now." (A face in a group photo.)

"That component is critical, but now we'll take a look at the overall performance of the circuit." (A circuit diagram example.)

"I'm sure you'll agree that such detail is important, but let's turn now to another aspect of design." (A blueprint example.)

### Other Options?

PowerPoint allows you to use an arrow pointer during a presentation. From your presentation position you would normally have a laptop or screen visible just below your line of sight to the audience. It isn't difficult to call up the pointer but once on screen it stays there, so park it to the side when it isn't needed. Apple's Keynote offers a similar option, but the arrow can be set to appear only when the mouse moves.

Personally I prefer the pen option. I can park it to the side, move it to circle or underline something, and park it again. The circle or underline is more easily visible and stays there as long as the slide is on screen. It isn't permanent and if I come back to that slide any annotations will be gone.

For most purposes, PowerPoint's built-in pointer and pen will be adequate, but there are situations where something more is needed. An interactive workshop could see the presenter adding notes to a screen image that needs to be retrieved later. To do this you need an additional piece of software. A touch stylus or an iPen will allow you to draw and annotate not just PowerPoint, but also Word, XL and other screens. There are several iPen options, and the software allows you to write and draw, change slides, and generally control your presentation. It takes a little getting used to, but is certainly a versatile and effective tool. Make sure the software is PC and Mac compatible.

There are several similar products on the market, and you should make sure you choose one that suits your needs. Try before you buy.

Rather than use an external pointer, you can focus attention on part of a text or image by using options within PowerPoint and Keynote.

Consider a list of six headings, of which you want to highlight three. A change of color of those three would be useful. Make your first text box as usual, and then copy it. Change the color of the three headings, and superimpose it precisely on the first text box. Now arrange the build order so that the first appears, showing all six, and then the second, showing the three in a different color. This can be done on click, or can appear after a timed delay.

With an image, you can superimpose circles or arrows in a similar way. Have the main image appear first, and then have circles, arrows or other secondary images appear on click or after a delay.

## 6.12 WORKING WITH THE DIGITAL PROJECTOR

**An Essential and Ubiquitous Modern Tool**

More and more presentations involve the combination of a laptop and a data projector, mainly using Keynote or PowerPoint.

A major benefit is the ability to have your presentation on a laptop, tablet, or even on a phone, connected to a projector. The laptop option allows you to easily see the projected image on its screen, so that you don't have to turn away from the audience to see it, and you are able to use remote control. The tablet or phone option also allows you to stay facing your audience, but doesn't usually allow for remote control. If using a laptop, make sure there will be a table of some sort for it. Tablets and phones can be hand-carried, so you can move around, but with the risk of losing the connecting cord. Cord free connections are increasingly available — a WiFi connection to the laptop, or a Bluetooth connection to the projector. A range of attachments is available for mounting tablets and phones on tables, lecterns, or mike stands.

The two key factors in a projector are the light output, and the focal length of the lens. Knowing something about any projector provided for you is useful.

Light output is measured in lumens. For any projector, making the projected image smaller will make it brighter, but perhaps not big enough for clarity.

A low output of around 1,000 to 1,200 lumens will be adequate in small rooms, but will likely need some dimming of ambient light such as closing the curtains and switching off any lights near the screen. Anything over 2,000 lumens should be fine in daylight or in brightly lit rooms, and will give a big image for large groups.

First, make sure the projector is safely positioned on a stable platform. Use a solid table rather than a folding one which might be more likely to move, making your projected image wobble. If using a media trolley, be sure to engage any brakes, or otherwise immobilize it. (More than once I've had to call on gaffa tape to secure a trolley.)

Try to fill the screen with a clear, square, straight image with no keystoning. And of course, in focus. The last thing you want to do is walk to the screen and point to it. You've lost eye contact with the audience, you're blinded by the projector, and you've become part of the screen, and of the image projected onto it. Definitely a no-no. Better to use a laser pointer, or use the software — PowerPoint, etc. — to direct attention by using a circle or arrow (see Section 6.11).

A wide-angle lens with a short focal length means the projector can be closer to the screen, and if it has to be brought in and placed on a table or stand, that may be what you need. A longer focal length means the projector has to be further back from the screen, which needs more cable, and perhaps the use of an assistant. Either way, aim to fill the screen.

Reverse projection is used where space is tight, or at a conference booth where a screen needs to be right beside the passing public. With normal projection, passing traffic would cast shadows so the projector is behind the screen. Mirrors allow the projected image to be reversed so that it shows properly from the front. You might still come across reverse projection screens, but TV screens have almost completely replaced them.

A ceiling-mounted projector needs a little more preparation since you can't reach the lens to cover it while you set up. Set up the laptop and test the connection to the projector so you know it works. Then set up the laptop with the title page and use a keyboard command to blank the screen. In Keynote or PowerPoint, just press "B" to show a blank black screen. Press it again to resume. (Your remote control should also allow this — don't buy one that doesn't.) "W" has a similar effect but shows a white screen, which might be useful in some circumstances, for example if you want a little more light so that people can take notes, or so that you can see if there are questions.

Ceiling-mounted projectors tend to be in the center line of a room, projecting to a screen on the back wall. The advantage of a ceiling mount is that the projected image angles down and you are less likely to wander into its path and cast a huge shadow. They are also likely to be properly set up, focused, and with no keystoning — but check! The snag is that a central screen narrows your options for audience layout.

A ceiling-mounted projector usually has a remote control for simple things such as switching it on and off. I once turned up to a venue — a church hall — where the remote control could not be found. It was locked away and nobody had a key. Fortunately the device was mounted so that the top, with the on/off switch, faced downwards. Standing on a chair, I used a microphone stand with a boom arm fully extended to reach and prod the switch thus saving the day.

Another problem presented itself when the projection system in a conference room was on. The laptop arrived and was duly connected. Nothing happened. We checked alternative connection paths. Nothing. Apparently, the system had to be switched on with the laptop already connected so that the system could "see" the laptop. A quick restart — problem solved and another lesson learned.

Which takes us to connecting to a projector. Older projectors used VGA, but modern machines use HDMI. A conference venue or hotel will usually have the relevant connectors, but it is essential to check. My usual kit includes a little black box to convert HDMI to VGA for older projectors. Earlier, I used to carry a VGA to HDMI box, but rarely use it now.

While using a cable connection is usually the only way to connect to a ceiling-mounted projector, you might have the option of using a streaming stick to connect to a flat-screen TV. This small device plugs into an HDMI input on the TV, and works via an app on your smartphone or tablet. The cheapest of them may be more difficult to work with and provide a slightly fuzzy screen image, but if you are comfortable with the technology, it's worth considering. Otherwise, you might prefer to stay safe with cable connections.

Software is now available to enable remote control of a laptop presentation from a smart phone or tablet. These usually require the laptop and smartphone to be on the same WiFi network. Hotels, libraries and conference centers usually have this available, but not always. One way around it is to take along your own WiFi network, e.g., an Airport Express. It doesn't need a connection to the internet. You just set it up to allow the two devices to pair and converse. Do that well before the start.

At the end of a presentation, if the projector is to be packed away, make sure it cools down before it is moved. This extends bulb life. Most will require the off switch to be pressed twice (for confirmation), and an indicator light will show, or the fan will continue to run, until the temperature is down to an acceptable level.

The need for portability has brought a new range of micro projectors to the market. Some of these are small enough to fit in a shirt pocket. They have much lower light outputs than their larger cousins, but are useful for small groups where a small image size is important and lower quality images will suffice.

**Digital Projector**

| | |
|---|---|
| Availability | Widely available but expensive.<br><br>Ceiling mounted projectors not always easy to operate – don't assume focus is correct. |
| Portability | Good – most are light enough to be carried quite easily. |
| Power | AC voltage. |
| Positioning | Needs a screen, but a light-colored wall can be used if necessary. |
| Visibility | Clearly visible in normal lighting, but always improved in lower light, especially near the screen.<br><br>Allows you to face the audience as you write. |
| Versatility | Handles text and graphics, audio and video.<br><br>Works with PowerPoint, Keynote, Google Slides, etc.<br><br>Often has zoom lens.<br><br>Often has keystone adjustment built in. |

*TABLE 9*

**Remote Controls**

A good remote control for your laptop is a great investment. The remote control enables you to change slides in PowerPoint without having to stand over the laptop keyboard. Most will work over the standard Bluetooth range of 10 meters or 30 feet. If you are a natural mover, or if movement is essential to your presentation, you need a remote control.

Some use AA or AAA batteries, which I prefer because they are more widely available. Others use coin shaped batteries such as the CR2032. Whichever you choose, always have spare batteries with you.

Make sure the forward and back controls are easy to find and use, and make sure there is a button to give you the blank screen for those occasions when you need to draw the audience back to you. With a little practice, you can operate the remote control without having to look at it.

Almost as important is a good carry case, with places for the remote, the USB plug-in, and spare batteries.

## 6.13    USING A WHITEBOARD

The basic whiteboard is just that. A white board on which one could write with colored pens. It has advantages over its ancestor, the blackboard or chalkboard, in that it is dust free, and has the same color profile as writing on paper. Colored pens are used to write on it, and the board can be cleared with a felt pad similar to the duster used on a chalkboard. However it retains the disadvantages that the presenter has to turn away from the audience to write on it, and unlike the flip chart, there is just one "page" at a time. For small groups, the whiteboard is often used a scribble pad, as is the flip chart.

Using a whiteboard is similar to the technique of using a chalkboard or flip chart. All three lend themselves to freehand writing and drawing, but the whiteboard doesn't allow for the "ghost" image which can be used on a chalkboard or flip chart.

A crucial factor is the pen. Fine lines aren't too clear, so use chisel point pens. Permanent ink can be removed, but with some effort, so make sure you use dry erase marker pens.

### Electronic Whiteboard

Modern technology brings us electronic whiteboards, also referred to as digital or interactive whiteboards. These are essentially images projected onto touchscreens. Files (text, audio, video, etc.) can be imported from elsewhere, and the proprietary software provides a range of drawing tools, file management and selection capabilities, etc. The software is usually straightforward and easy to navigate, but if you don't use such facilities regularly, make sure you create an opportunity to practice.

Although developed initially for classroom use, the combination of projected image and touchscreen means that the presenter is often standing in the projected image, which is not ideal. The viewing angle is not always wide enough for those at the side of the room, and audio output may be insufficient for those at the back of the room.

Modern smartboards are a further development. Instead of a projected image, a smartboard uses a high-resolution touch-screen TV display. Once again, to use the touchscreen, the presenter has to stand in front of the image, making it hard for some of the audience to see it. This makes it more suited to collaborative working or presentations, since even the largest can be hard to see from the back of a room. This doesn't apply to any online audience. The software is usually straightforward and easy to navigate, but if you don't use a smartboard regularly, make sure you create an opportunity to practice.

## 6.14 DEALING WITH DISASTER

**How do you react when it doesn't go to plan?**

Few presentation disasters are fatal. You can usually succeed if you keep smiling, and have a clear idea of your main purpose. The best insurance against disaster is good preparation, but you'll know the full truth of that only when disaster strikes.

First, let's look at some general disaster scenarios that might arise:

THE POWER FAILS AND YOUR EQUIPMENT IS DEAD.

As the person 'on stage' you are the first person people will look to. Equipment failure means you have to fall back on your plan — aren't you glad you made one? Simply discuss the points you want to make and reach your conclusion. If the PA is also dead, you have to raise your voice, without shouting.

THE LIGHTS FAIL.

In daylight, and a room with windows, this isn't a serious problem. At night, or in a windowless room, if the lights go out, there will be emergency lighting for the exits, and you might be able to continue, but make a point of calmly asking for someone to investigate the problem.

YOU FIND YOU HAVE 10 MINUTES INSTEAD OF THE 20 YOU PLANNED FOR.

You can't just talk faster — that creates a disaster in itself. This is where your planning really pays off. Remind yourself of your prime purpose and focus on it. Decide quickly what percentage of 10 minutes each part of your presentation should take. Keep your eye on the clock and limit yourself to the key point in each section.

YOU WALK IN TO PRESENT TO A SMALL GROUP, AND ARE OFFERED A COMFORTABLE-LOOKING SEAT.

Thank them for the consideration, but indicate that you'd feel more comfortable standing. Alternatively, sit down now, and as you begin your introduction, rise to your feet and continue from there. Once on your feet you're unlikely to be asked to sit down again. From a standing position you can manage your notes and aids much better, breathe more easily, see your audience more clearly, and project your voice better.

YOU EXPECT TO SPEAK TO THREE PEOPLE AND ARRIVE TO FIND 15.

If handouts were part of your plan, they aren't now. If a flip chart and pens are available, you might be able to use it to put up your main points, but no more. Otherwise there's no problem. Remember that you are the expert. Stay confident. Keep smiling. Stick to your presentation plan, but ask yourself, why are these extra people here? You probably should ask them since the answer may require a change in the purpose of your presentation.

THE FIRE ALARM GOES OFF DURING YOUR PRESENTATION.

Assuming it's a false alarm and you're going to get back in, try to seek out the organizer or chairperson as you head for the assembly area and arrange to resume. Assume that the disruption to the day's schedule will allow no more than that you move straight to your final point, and try to insist that you be allowed to do that. Point out that from the organizer's point of view it will help to restore a little continuity to the day, and give them a little more time to brief the next speaker and reschedule the day.

Next, some personal problems:

YOU LOSE YOUR TRAIN OF THOUGHT IN MID-SENTENCE.

Smile, say "Excuse me." check your planner, and start the sentence or the point again. Keep in mind that everyone in the room has lost track of an idea at least once. People generally want you to succeed and are sympathetic. Keep smiling and try to appear confident.

YOUR THROAT DRIES OUT.

Stop, preferably at the end of a sentence. Say 'excuse me' and reach for the glass of water. If there isn't one handy, ask if someone can fetch one for you. Most people will be sympathetic to your plight and will help. Continue when you are ready.

YOU DROP YOUR NOTES OR OTHER ITEMS ON THE FLOOR.

Make a joke about your clumsiness, pick them up and take a moment to put them in order. (Now is the time to be grateful you have numbered them, and to remind yourself to use a ring binder in the future.) Alternatively, make a joke of it — you've just done it to make sure everyone is still awake.

YOU COME PREPARED WITH A FLIP CHART TO FIND THEY WANT YOU IN THE MIDDLE OF A LONG CONFERENCE TABLE AND SOMEONE ELSE IS TO HANDLE THE FLIP CHART

Give polite thanks but state that you would rather handle your own flip chart, take the initiative. Suggest that your audience will find it easier to see you if you move to the end of the table, and start moving as you say it. Most people will find it hard to say no to you.

YOU COME PREPARED WITH A POWERPOINT OR KEYNOTE PRESENTATION BUT THERE IS NO PROJECTOR.

Can one be summoned or can you be rescheduled to go on later?

If not, turn to your planner and quickly identify the crucial visuals that absolutely have to be seen. Can you draw them quickly, perhaps on a flip chart, and show them that way? Can you make your point and achieve your purpose in some other way — perhaps an activity of some kind?

If visuals are a crucial element and there is no way to show them, the best that you can do may be to offer your conclusion, and use a Q&A session to allow the audience to explore the supporting evidence.

YOU EXPERIENCE A WARDROBE MALFUNCTION

'Wardrobe malfunctions' are a fact of life. For men, the fly unzipped, or the lower shirt buttons coming undone; for women, the unbuttoned blouse, the skirt tucked into the underwear after a bathroom visit — you know the list of possibilities. I've had it happen, and you will too at some point.

Nearly everyone in your audience has had one of these at some point in their life, perhaps in a similar circumstance, so there's a strong degree of sympathy that you can work on.

The worst thing you can do is to let any embarrassment show, and struggle to remedy the malfunction. That highlights the problem and is a total diversion for the audience.

The best thing you can do is make light of it as you quickly and discreetly remedy the malfunction. Try to make them remember how you handled it rather than the malfunction itself.

"Well, excuse me, one more adjustment to make."

"Thankyou — that was a very generous lunch/dinner."

"Well I'm sure you didn't expect to see as much of me as that!"

"Please remind me later to place a call to my tailor!"

Finally, some audience problems:

SEVERAL PEOPLE START A CONVERSATION WHILE YOU ARE SPEAKING.

Stop when you can.

Ask if there are questions or if you can do anything to clarify a point.

If they don't stop, continue your presentation but try to move nearer to them. You become more visually intrusive, and that may stop them.

Lower your voice a little or pause, so that their conversation becomes more obvious.

Hope that someone else will stop them for you.

THE KEY PERSON OR DECISION MAKER HAS TO LEAVE BEFORE YOU HAVE REACHED YOUR KEY POINTS.

If you follow the old rule "Tell them what you are going to tell them, tell them, tell them what you told them," you won't get caught this way. Always mention your main point and major supporting points within the first few minutes of any presentation. If you are using visuals, you always have a visual that has the main point and the key points. If, however, you have made the fatal error of trying to save the key point for last, and the decision maker must leave, ask for a moment to summarize (most people will give you a moment if you ask with a smile) and state, in one sentence, the one point you want the decision maker to remember and, if you have a chance, the two arguments that best support that point.

YOU ARRIVE AND ARE TOLD THE KEY PERSON OR DECISION MAKER CAN'T BE THERE.

If the decision maker can't be there, someone present will be responsible for reporting to him or her. Ask yourself, "What, in one sentence, do I want that reporter to say?" (What do I want the decision maker to do?) It will not be, "He told us about..." It will be a message, for example "We should use ... because it is within our budget and meets our engineering requirements." Then be sure you state that sentence, as you want it repeated, at the beginning and at the end of your presentation.

SOMEONE ASKS ABOUT SOMETHING YOU PLAN TO DISCUSS IN DETAIL LATER.

Answer the question briefly, and say you plan to go into detail later. If the questioner is the decision maker, ask if the short answer is sufficient for now. Do not ask people to wait until you reach the point at which you originally planned to cover the material. If you do, everyone will focus on the unanswered question instead of listening. In a meeting setting, don't ask people to hold their questions until the end. Making that request suggests you are not confident enough to deal with interruptions.

YOU PLAN TO WORK THROUGH A HANDOUT PAGE BY PAGE BUT PEOPLE ARE MOVING AHEAD AT THEIR OWN PACE.

The risk in giving people printed material is that they will read it at their own pace. If possible, don't provide handouts until after the presentation is over. If you must walk through a printed booklet, tell people what it contains and give them an idea of where different parts are located before you begin. If possible, hold your copy up on an easel and point to parts of charts or graphs. People are also more likely to stay with you if you occasionally say, "And you can see on page ___ that…" If the decision maker insists on moving ahead quickly, you'll do best to pick up the pace, perhaps skip pages, and, if necessary, focus on the pages that are important to him or her. (If you are going to hand out materials, don't try to bury anything at the end such as costs or fees. If people don't find what they want at the beginning, they tend to go immediately to the end.)

There are many more potential pitfalls, and the point is that in presentations, as in so many other areas of life, it is best to hope for the best but plan for the worst. Without a plan or some forethought any of these situations could be disastrous. Handling a disaster well may not make a huge impression (it might not even be noticed), but mishandling it certainly will.

# 7

# Postliminary

*Postliminary: The work of a presenter doesn't end with the closing remarks of the presentation, or the end of the questions. There is more to do, especially if you are a regular presenter, or aspire to be a professional speaker/presenter.*

## 7.1 EVALUATING YOUR PRESENTATION

**Did it work? Did you achieve your purpose?**

You've found your way to this chapter, possibly having read all the preceding chapters. Or perhaps not.

Either way, it all comes down to delivery.

You're on. Perhaps you've been able to make an entrance with style, in a way that concentrates audience attention. This can be as simple as walking on, rather than being there and rising to your feet.

Every eye is on you, and every ear is ready for you.

The trite saying applies — preparation prevents poor performance. Preparing your material and yourself is crucial. Practice if you can. You might not be able to practice for delivery on short notice, but you can take it home and practice it afterwards. Building up your delivery skills will help you with the next one.

With experience, any skill develops. Your presentations will improve as you do more of them, and the preparation becomes easier.

Don't forget to leave time for questions.

And evaluation where possible, even if just for yourself. Sometimes you will be evaluated (e.g., a college presentation or a job interview) but it's always useful, where possible, to gather feedback in order to improve.

### Key Evaluation Questions
*How was it? Did I succeed in my purpose? What can I do better next time?*

### Evaluation Forms
For a regular presenter, evaluation is crucial for two reasons.

1. It's the essential feedback needed to show that the purpose has been achieved, and to suggest where improvements might be made.
2. It provides a body of evidence showing the competence of the presenter which can be used in marketing.

You know it's important, but typically the return rate for evaluation forms is low. At the end, people are keen to go for coffee or a meal, a bathroom break or the train home.

When we are given a gift, we feel indebted to the giver. Without really knowing it, we feel uncomfortable with this indebtedness, and feel urged to cancel the debt, often against our better judgment. This is known to the psychologists as the rule of reciprocity, and is widely used by service industries. When we get a candy with our restaurant bill, research shows that we give a slightly bigger tip than when we do not. If the server adds an extra candy and a big smile, we usually give even more.

As a presenter, you can use this not only in a presentation, but also to bring in those evaluation forms. I once did a presentation to a fairly small group, and gave everyone an evaluation form in a stamped addressed envelope. The return was 90%, and the bonus was that my name and address were available to each participant for far longer than if I'd just given out business cards. Since then I've used the technique from time to time.

Evaluation can be done in many different ways, so here are a few points to consider.

### Evaluation Questions
Evaluation needs to ask questions that people can answer and that inform them and you about the effectiveness of the presentation in achieving its declared purpose.

| Purpose of Presentation | Questions that might be asked |
|---|---|
| Information giving | Were you given enough information?<br>Was the information useful?<br>Was this the information you needed? |
| Persuading | Did you agree with what was suggested?<br>Did you agree with (specific point)? |
| Educating/Informing | Do you feel you now have a better understanding of...?<br>Do you still have questions about...? |
| Training | Do you have any remaining questions about...?<br>Do you now feel competent to....? |

*TABLE 10. EVALUATION QUESTIONS*

### Evaluation Answers

Before setting up an evaluation form, ask yourself how the information will be processed. Simple questions — were you given enough information — will give you yes/no answers, which can be counted. They are also easy for the audience members to do, and so you should get more returns.

Unless you have a way of requiring evaluations from each participant (e.g., trade a completed evaluation form for a lunch ticket), you probably have to strike a balance between ease of completion for the participant and the usefulness of information for you.

The following examples should help you.

- - - - - - - - - - - - - - - - - - - - - - - - - - - - - - - - - - - - - - - - - - - - - - - - - - - - - - - - - - - - - -

### Example One
*Please complete the following evaluation form before you leave.*

1. *Did you enjoy the presentation?*      *Yes*      *Uncertain*      *No*
2. *Was the speaker clearly audible?*      *Yes*      *Uncertain*      *No*
3. *Were the graphics clearly visible?*      *Yes*      *Uncertain*      *No*
4. *Were the workshop sessions long enough?*      *Yes*      *Uncertain*      *No*
5. *Were the coffee breaks long enough?*      *Yes*      *Uncertain*      *No*
6. *Was the seating comfortable?*      *Yes*      *Uncertain*      *No*
7. *Would you like to suggest any improvements?*

*Thanks for your help in completing this form.*

- - - - - - - - - - - - - - - - - - - - - - - - - - - - - - - - - - - - - - - - - - - - - - - - - - - - - - - - - - - - - -

Few examples are as bad as this (and yes, it's a real example I collected), but you've probably seen many that come close.

Three options are given, and the middle option tells you nothing.

The questions indicate a concern for comfort levels and enjoyment, which is somewhat pointless unless this is one of a repeated series of events at the same venue. How does anyone judge if the workshop sessions were long enough? For a one-off event, can you really use this information?

The open invitation to suggest improvements invites all manner of comments, including the unseemly!

The form is impersonal — it could be any event, anywhere, and so there is little incentive to participate.

---

**Example Two**
*Topic: Internal Communications*
*Client: Widget Company*

*Your feedback is valuable. Please give me your considered opinion on the following:*

| | | | | | |
|---|---|---|---|---|---|
| 1. | *Was the seating comfortable?* | *Definite yes* | *Yes* | *No* | *Definite no* |
| 2. | *Could you hear clearly?* | *Definite yes* | *Yes* | *No* | *Definite no* |
| 3. | *Could you see clearly?* | *Definite yes* | *Yes* | *No* | *Definite no* |
| 4. | *Was the presentation informative?* | *Definite yes* | *Yes* | *No* | *Definite no* |
| 5. | *Did you have unanswered questions?* | *Definite yes* | *Yes* | *No* | *Definite no* |
| 6. | *Would you be happy to attend another presentation made by the same person?* | *Definite yes* | *Yes* | *No* | *Definite no* |
| 7. | *Do you have any comments that would help us to improve on future presentations?* | | | | |

*Thanks for completing the form.*
*Your feedback helps us to maintain the highest standards for which we constantly strive.*
*N E Body*
*The Presentation Company*

---

This is much better.
The form is specific to the event and to the client.
The form indicates the importance of the response.
Four options avoid fence sitting. Respondents have to come down on one side or the other.
The first three questions address personal experience and indicate a concern for the individual.
The first six questions allow for responses to be added up.
Questions four and five invite the individual to reflect on what they learned, and encourages them to consider further action to get their questions answered.

Question six invites an overall reaction to the presenter.

Question seven invites purposeful comment.

The responses can be added up quickly for interpretation.

The footnote reminds participants of the value of their comments, and of your (or your company's) respect for quality.

The name and contact details remind people that someone really will read it.

---

**Example Three** (also anonymous but also real)
*Rate the Group Presentation (5= Excellent; 1= Poor; NA= not applicable)*
*Comments would be very helpful.*

*Group Number: _____ Group Topic: _____*

1. *Introduction: Did the introduction capture your interest; was necessary background given; was a clear purpose conveyed?*

2. *Content: Did the group support their points; was the supporting material relevant, up to date?*

3. *Visual Aids: Were visual aids used effectively and appropriately, carefully prepared?*

4. *Conclusion: Were key points reinforced; was a sense of closure provided; if appropriate, was a course of action proposed?*

5. *Delivery: Were the speakers natural, enthusiastic; did they speak clearly; were appropriate gestures, posture, expressions used?*

6. *Discussion: Were questions answered accurately, clearly, effectively?*

7. *Overall Rating*

8. *General Comments (use back):*

---

This has a few flaws.

- Anonymous: Who is presenting what, and to whom?
- Not easy to fill in: Circling the numbers 1 through 5 would be easier.
- Multiple questions are asked each time: So which is/are being answered?
- On what basis is the overall rating to be made?
- The invitation to make "general comments" is too vague.

It's hard to see just how this could be processed, and impossible to see what useful information any processing could yield. Anyone who looks at it closely will wonder why they should bother to complete it.

A simple improvement would be to separate out the individual questions, and provide a 1-4 scale so that people could quickly circle or check the number.

*Can you think of other improvements that would make evaluation more user-friendly, and allow quicker and easier processing?*

## 7.2 FINALE

**It's over, but you haven't finished yet!**
You reach the end, and enjoy the applause. It's a great feeling, and you might find it addictive. Many people do. The level of addiction will depend on you, but even a mild addiction means you'll want to do this again.

You've handled the questions, and it's time to leave the floor. You still have work to do.

There are people to be thanked, ranging from the colleagues who listened, technicians who helped you, any other speakers who shared the platform with you, the organizer(s) who booked you, and anyone else who contributed to your performance and to your success.

Your various aids and items of equipment have to be collected and repacked ready to take away. Some take the "shovel it in and sort it later" approach, and if that works for you then go ahead. If time is short, it may be necessary. The risk is that something is overlooked and left behind. I find it better to have a system. Cables and power leads are carefully coiled, notes and paperwork tidied, and specific things go in specific boxes. It's easy to check that everything is there. When I get back to base, little needs to be repacked or checked, and most things go straight back into their storage slot. Batteries are removed from devices wherever possible, ready for new batteries next time.

Back at base there's the "thank you" letter to whoever hired you, and usually some evaluation to be processed.

Inevitably there are lessons to be learned from any notes you made to yourself at the time.

Those questions from the audience that you took away to answer later have to be researched and dealt with.

Final expenses may have to be calculated and an invoice to be issued.

Put a note into your diary to follow up with some promotional literature some weeks later, so that your name is more likely to come up when they want another presentation or workshop, or just put a 'thank you' note on the office noticeboard.

If the most satisfying experience in presentation is the applause at the end, the second most satisfying is when the check arrives, and the third is when that call comes through to ask you back.

I hope this book helps you to have all three experiences as often as possible.

# 8

# Using Checklists

*Checklists – the more often you expect to be providing presentations,*
*the more useful checklists are likely to be.*

Do you have the information about where and when, what you have to do, what equipment you need, the correct cables and cords, enough batteries, etc.? These checklists are provided as a starting point and are based on the ones I use. Appendix F has printable versions. You are unlikely to use all of them as they are. Develop them into whatever will best help you and your own approach to presentations, the equipment you have available, etc.

## 8.1 AGREEMENT CHECKLIST

This is the checklist you keep handy and grab when the phone rings or that email comes in. You might not be able to complete it right away, but you should capture the essential information as soon as you can, leaving you free to work on developing the presentation, checking what equipment might be needed, etc.

**AGREEMENT HORROR STORY**

The presenter walked into the hotel, bag of equipment in one hand, and flip chart tucked under the other arm. He asked the reception staff for directions to the room where the meeting is to be held, and was met with blank looks. Another member of staff arrived, and solved the problem. That meeting was last night — they were looking for you. *Yes, it happened to me. I had been asked to stand in for someone else who passed me the details, but I hadn't checked those details or visited the venue, and it was embarrassing. (So please don't tell anybody else. Please.)*

PRESENTATION PURPOSE
– to engage and inform audience

THE PROBLEM
– poor planning and preparation

RESULT
– zero engagement and information

SOLUTIONS
– check date
– check time
– check venue

## 8.2 WORKING SAFELY

Presentations are not high on anyone's list of hazardous events, but there are a few potential risks and you need to be aware of them, and minimize them. I've been caught out with an over-weight suitcase. It had wheels, but lifting it up steps proved to be my downfall, resulting in a sprained arm. Since then, I travel lighter, and ask for help when I need it. The last thing you want to do is give yourself an unnecessary injury just before a presentation.

At a presentation venue, do you always know where the emergency exits are? Or what the fire alarm sounds like? In some places you are required to start an event by pointing out where the emergency exits and assembly areas are, and indicate what the fire alarm sound is. Sometimes that duty will fall to you. In an emergency, as the person on stage, or out front, you will be the first person that people will look to, and expect you handle the situation.

You might find yourself about to walk onto a stage littered with audio and power cables which present a tripping hazard. How you handle that can make a big difference to you, to the event, and to the organizers. I'd suggest you go ahead very carefully, but make your point afterwards, politely and calmly.

This is no definitive checklist that will prevent any and every accident. Nor will using a checklist guarantee safety, but it will help.

## 8.3 PRESENTER'S PLANNING CHECKLIST

This starts with the information from the Initial Agreement checklist, so you know the where and when. Then, as you develop the presentation, you can check off the resources needed. This checklist is mainly a reminder of techniques and good practices, e.g. making good eye contact with the audience.

## 8.4 ESSENTIAL PRESENTATION ITEMS

**Do you have all the kit you need?**

The Presenter's kit checklist is another inventory of what you have available. Some of it might be your own and some might belong to your employing company, but you need to list it to remind you that it's there when you need it. You should also add a note of where to find it or who to ask for it. You should be able to check your own equipment, but if some of it comes from a departmental store, or someone else's office, make sure you acquire it in time to check it too.

## 8.5 VENUE CHECKLIST

This is a checklist such as might be used by a hotel or by an organization that books presenters from time to time. If they ask these questions as they go through their checklist, that should be reassuring — they know what they're doing. If they don't ask, you should do the checking, and you might even offer them your version of the checklist. I once left one of mine with a hotel that had come under new ownership and was developing the conference side of their business — they appreciated the help.

# ⑨
# An Example in Detail

*This is an example of a presentation in practice, from request, through planning to delivery. It shows how I tackled the topic. At each step, ask yourself "Was that the best thing to do? Would I do it differently?"*

"Could I do a one-hour presentation on the keys to fundraising?" was the question. The audience was to be a group of teachers undergoing a technology development course.

Of course I could. It would be two weeks away in a university meeting room with space for the group but little more.

The purpose was both to provide information and offer encouragement to the teachers as they sought additional funding for their schools and their students.

First, I pulled out my planning checklist to check a few details. I knew the when and where, and something about the audience. No audio support would be needed, and the room had no lighting problems. I had a little research to do on the topic, mainly updating existing information and acquiring some details relevant to the specific location.

The title easily became a question, so the conclusion was also already written.

*Title: What are the three keys to successful fundraising?*
*Conclusion: These are the three keys to unlocking funds for your students.*

Next I drafted out some subtopics:

- *Key 1 – Know your request*
- *Key 2 – Know your recipient*
- *Key 3 – Know your donor*

As I did so it became apparent that these teachers needed to take away a great deal of information and so a handout would become essential. My role would be to clarify the subtopics, give examples, and generate some motivation. An enthusiastic, upbeat approach would be necessary. To put it all in a realistic context I'd need stories. Lots of stories, but in the end I used only two.

Since this was a technology group I could use Keynote and offer copies of the presentation via email. While the main information would be in a handout, I could use Keynote for basic headings while I added detail. Here's the Keynote flow — simple, basic, and focused.

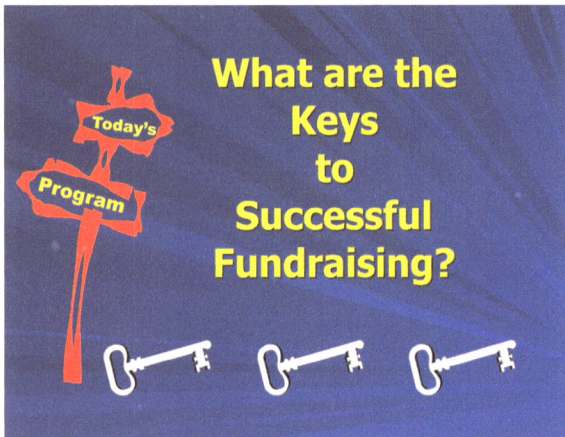

*Figure 72*

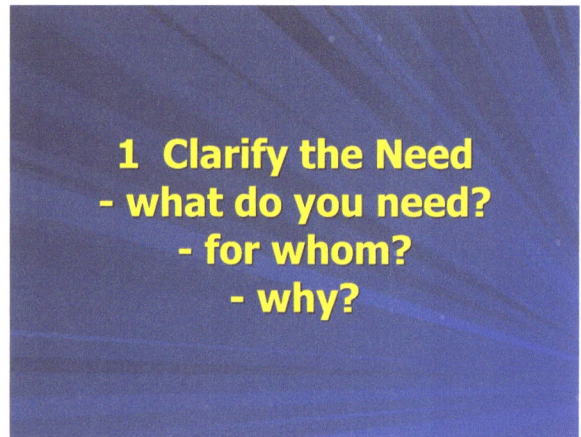

*Figure 73*

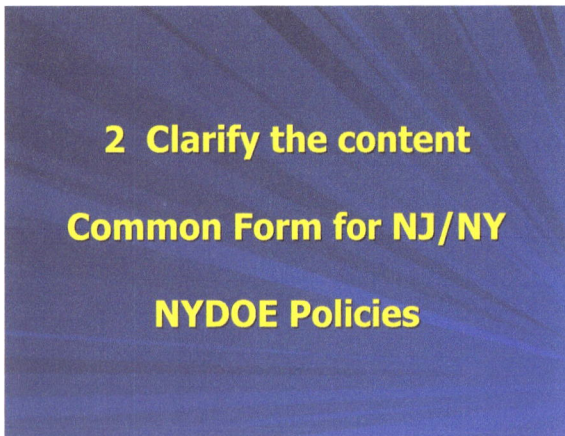

*Figure 74*

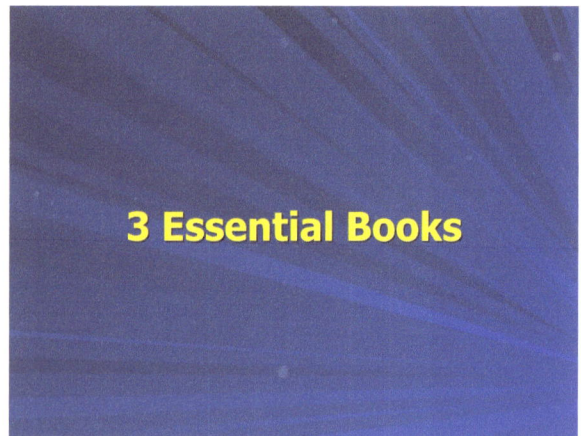

*Figure 75*

An Example in Detail

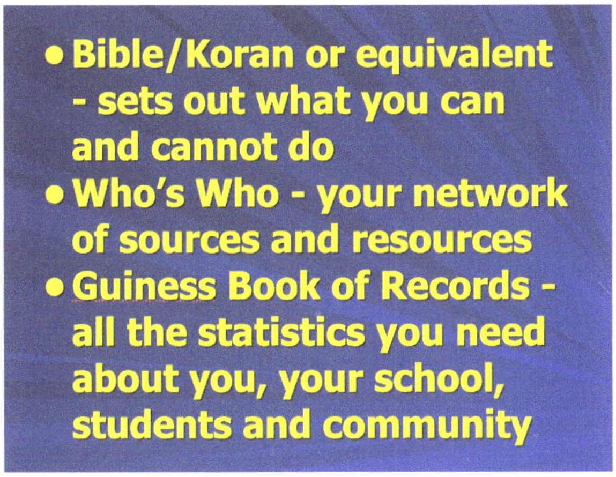

- **Bible/Koran or equivalent - sets out what you can and cannot do**
- **Who's Who - your network of sources and resources**
- **Guiness Book of Records - all the statistics you need about you, your school, students and community**

*Figure 76*

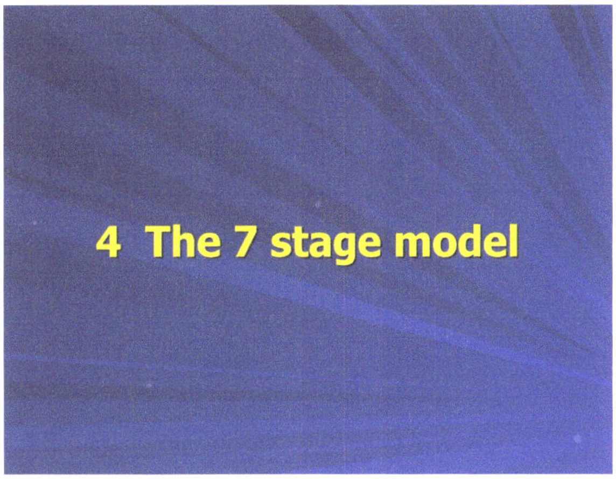

**4  The 7 stage model**

*Figure 77*

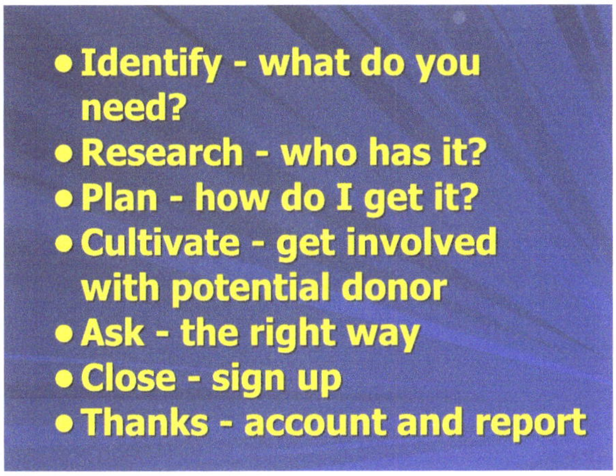

- **Identify - what do you need?**
- **Research - who has it?**
- **Plan - how do I get it?**
- **Cultivate - get involved with potential donor**
- **Ask - the right way**
- **Close - sign up**
- **Thanks - account and report**

*Figure 78*

**5    Action**

*Figure 79*

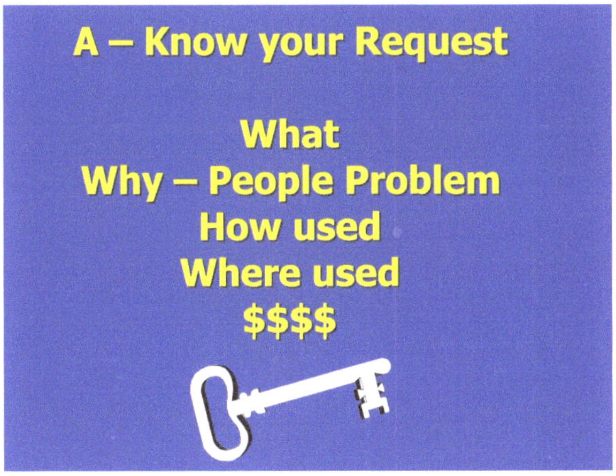

**A — Know your Request**

**What**
**Why — People Problem**
**How used**
**Where used**
**$$$$**

*Figure 80*

**B — Know your Recipient**

**Sizes**
**Catchment area**
**Achievements**
**Needs**

*Figure 81*

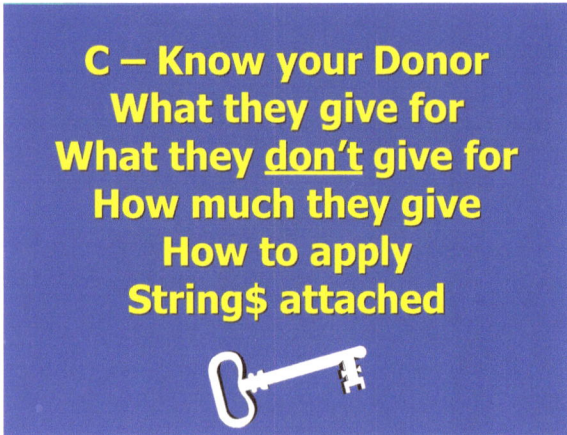

*Figure 82*

*Figure 83*

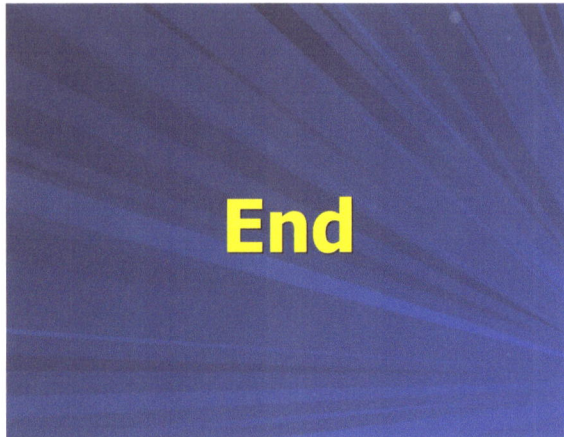

*Figure 84*

(An overhead projector would have worked just as well, but this would be too much work to handle on a flip chart.)

Did you spot the spelling error? Not too serious, but I missed it at the time, so I've left it in.

Two slides break the Rule of Seven, but I made the text as big as I could to ensure readability.

The three books could have been on separate pages, but it made sense to have the seven stages all on one slide.

The handout contained a range of funding sources available to teachers, and sources of information about four other donors. Teachers already knew most of the sources available to them, and so this presentation focused on how to make successful bids.

For a presentation as short and compact as this I might not always use a planner, but when I do I prefer a landscape version. That makes it easy to place in a presentation folder or a ring binder. In this case I used a ring binder, with my title showing to the audience, and my planner facing me so it was clearly visible. To hold it together, I used my ID lanyard. Time targets along the foot of the planner helped me to stay on course.

An Example in Detail

The room was full, but there was space for the projector and laptop. My title (Figure 86) was on a flip chart at the side and I allowed myself a little creative scope to help make it more memorable. The keys and dollar signs were echoed in the slides.

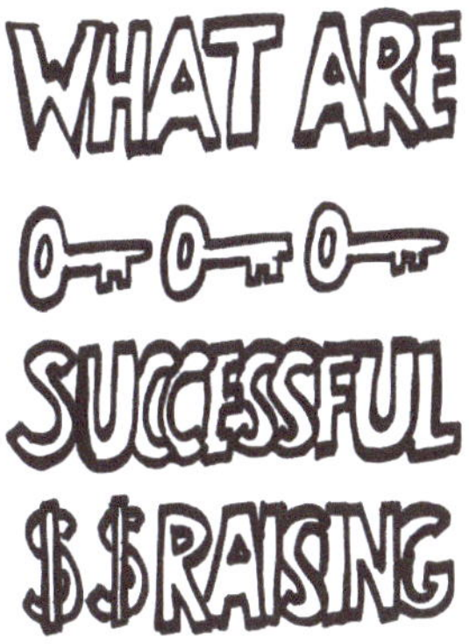

Figure 85. Title

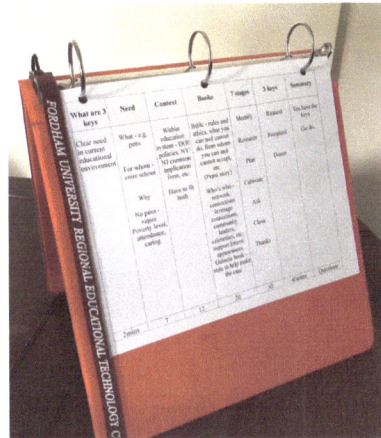

Figure 86. Planner page

This lettering style is easier to do than it looks, and more legible from a distance than single stroke letters. Sometimes I use a version with rounded letters. I developed the planner (Table 11, overlead) and had the printed page in a ring binder, propped up on the table (Figure 86). The times are time elapsed, not a time allocation. I sometimes set my phone beside the planner with the stopwatch application running to check my progress, but in this case there was a wall clock at the back of the room.

As people arrived, I was able to chat with them and collect some ideas about their fund-raising needs, picking out a couple I could use in the presentation. I briefed a colleague. Once I had started, he placed a pile of handouts on a chair by the door for people to collect on the way out.

I had left time for questions at the end, but instead they came thick and fast during the presentation. Having time targets enabled me to recalculate on the fly, and still finish on time.

I worked from the headings in the planner, and recorded the presentation. This is what I said for the first slide.

*Let's say we need pens.*

*We need them for whom? Our students? Too vague.*

*Be more precise. We need pens for 560 students in our school, and we want to be able to give every student four pens per school year. That's more precise. Much better. Yes?*

*Why do we need them? Because they don't have pens. Too vague and there's no strength of appeal. Let's put a human face on the problem. Let's make it a people problem.*

*We need them because 60% of our families are below the poverty level, and almost 50% are single-parent families. Faced with the choice of buying pens or food, parents choose food. Giving our students a pen is a gift that they will appreciate. For many, just getting to school is an achievement, and we want to encourage*

| What Are 3 Keys | Need | Context | Books | 7 Stages | 3 Keys | Summary |
|---|---|---|---|---|---|---|
| Clear need in current educational environment | What – e.g. pens<br><br>For whom – entire school<br><br>Why<br><br>No pens – vague<br><br>Poverty level, attendance, caring story | Within education system – DOE policies, NY / NJ common application form, etc.<br><br>Have to fit both | Bible – rules and ethics, what you can and cannot do, from whom you can and cannot accept, etc. (Pepsi story)<br><br>*Who's Who* – network, connections leverage connections, community leaders, celebrities, etc. support letters/appearances<br><br>*Guinness Book of Records* – statistics to help make the case | Identify<br><br>Research<br><br>Plan<br><br>Cultivate<br><br>Ask<br><br>Close<br><br>Thanks | Request<br><br>Recipient<br><br>Donor | You have the keys.<br><br>Go, do. |
| *2 mins* | *7* | *12* | *20* | *30* | *40 mins* | *Questions* |

*TABLE 11. PLANNER*

An Example in Detail

*and reward their social effort as well as their academic effort. We want to give them a small token to show we care, and to remove a small barrier to their progress.*

*Now our donor knows that we're not just asking for a resource, we're addressing a real social need for real people. Whatever resource you're asking for, make it a people problem, and show how their help can contribute to solving it.*

Can you imagine the delivery here?

Making eye contact with individuals as I asked them questions or set them challenges helped to focus their attention.

Dramatic pauses allowed them to place things in their own context, and invited nods of agreement.

Changes of pitch and speed helped to emphasize points, and support the encouragement I was trying to provide.

Two hundred words might normally take little more than a minute, but with pauses and a question or two, it easily became two.

At the end of the presentation, all the handouts were collected, and a few lingered to ask further questions.

I didn't carry out any specific evaluation, but the collection of handouts and the number and quality of questions suggested that the presentation had gone well. I felt that I had succeeded in my two purposes — providing information, and offering encouragement.

This was a simple presentation, with a clear aim and an interested audience. Perhaps the subject matter isn't familiar, but the context may be.

**How might you complete the presentation?**
**How would you approach a similar presentation?**

# Glossary

*Glossary – What do all those strange words mean?*
This is where to find out.

**A4**
A standard page size in Europe, roughly equivalent to the US letter size.
One A4 page is 29.7cm x 21.0cm, or 11.69 inches long and 8.27 inches wide.
A US Letter page is 11.0 inches long and 8.5 inches wide.

**Adaptor**
A device that converts from one connection type to another. For example, if you travel abroad, you're likely to need an adaptor to allow your electrical equipment to fit the local sockets. Audio adaptors can allow the 3.5mm jack output of your laptop to connect to the XLR input on professional equipment. See also convertor.

**AIFF**
A file format for audio. AIFF files are high quality, but take roughly 10mb per minute of audio.

**Audacity**
Audacity is free audio recording and processing software that is easy to use, and well supported by an online manual and help pages. Audacity can record and edit multitrack audio and works for Windows, Mac, OS X, GNU/Linux and other operating systems. The interface is translated into many languages. You can use Audacity to record live audio on a laptop, edit, and convert the file to a space-saving MP3 format.

## Audience

Those who receive your presentation. Depending on the situation, your audience could be just one person, or it could be a conference audience of hundreds.

## Audience Involvement Technique

Any technique that prompts the audience to do something as part of the presentation. Audience involvement techniques help to gain attention, can make the experience more memorable, and assist in achieving the purpose of the presentation.

## AV Aid (Audio Visual Aid)

Anything involving sight and sound (i.e., usually video) that a presenter can show to the audience to help make a point or increase understanding.

## Blu Tack

A handy reusable adhesive resembling putty or plasticine. Originally developed for holding posters on walls, Blu Tack and similar products have a range of other uses and should be part of any presenter's kit. Posters and other paperwork can be stuck on walls and removed without marking the surface. A lump on a lectern can be used to steady a laser pointer, thereby avoiding the distraction of demented bee syndrome.

## Bluetooth

Bluetooth is a short-range wireless technology. Bluetooth is commonly used for wireless keyboards and mice, and for remote controls for laptops. The most common form of Bluetooth has a range of around 10 meters or 30 feet. This makes it suitable for use in most classrooms, small meeting rooms, or stages. Bluetooth speakers can be fed audio from a laptop or phone to provide a small level of audio reinforcement. Some laptops and projectors can also be connected via Bluetooth for presentation purposes.

## Body Language

The way you position yourself reflects your unspoken intentions and feelings. We all understand a smile or a frown. We can usually tell when someone is impatient, or relaxed, even if they say nothing. As a presenter, you have to convey positive messages, not just by your speech, but by the way you interact with the audience, such as making eye contact with different people at different times, or leaning slightly toward the audience.

## Bongo Ties

Bongo ties are very strong rubber bands with a wooden or plastic toggle. Very useful for fastening coils of cable, and a host of other purposes. Carry a few with you to any presentation and it won't be long before you wonder how you ever did without them.

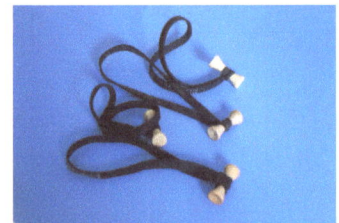

*Figure 87*

## Burn

Burning is the term used for writing data to a CD. The data can be files of any kind, including text, images, audio, video, etc.

## Carousel

A carousel is a circular holder of 35 mm slides, used in the Kodak Carousel range of slide projectors. For specific purposes where high-quality images are required, 35 mm slides may still be used.

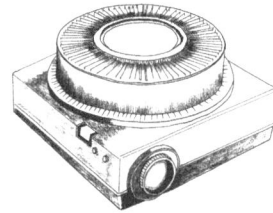

*Figure 88*

## Compact Disc (CD)

A format for recorded audio that is now less common as MP3 players have taken over. CDs typically have a capacity of 700mb, and can also store data such as text files, presentations, photos, spreadsheets, etc. CD-R refers to CDs to which data can be written once, and is then fixed. CD-RW means ReWriteable. Data can be written to the disc many times.

## CD-R

A Compact Disc that can be read only.

## Connector

A device that enables electrical circuits to be connected to each other. Examples include AC plugs to connect equipment to AC power, and audio connectors such as XLR, jack and phone plugs.

## Continuous Variable

Temperature is one example of a continuous variable. It changes smoothly up and down between different values and can be measured, but cannot be counted.

## Contract

A binding and enforceable business agreement.

## Convertor

A device, often in a little black box, that converts one form of signal to another, e.g., converting VGA signals to HDMI, and vice versa. Travelers between Europe and the USA may need a convertor to allow equipment to be used in the differing voltages. See also adaptor.

## Cueing

A process of identifying the required start point within a section of audio or video, and arranging playback to start at precisely that point.

## Demented Bee Syndrome

A term used to describe the wavering of a laser pointer's dot when held in an unsteady hand. A better technique is to move the dot back and forth as though to underline part of the image, or describe small circles to surround it. Alternatively, lean your hand against a table or lectern, or fasten the pointer in place with a lump of Blu Tack or plasticine.

## Digital Projector

A digital projector takes the VGA or HDMI output from your laptop, and projects it onto a screen so that an audience can see it. Most conference venues, hotels and schools will have their own, sometimes ceiling mounted so that you plug in somewhere close to hand and use a remote control. Focus and image size are usually set so the remote is really just for ON and OFF. Older projectors may still use VGA connection, but modern ones will have HDMI which offers a better-quality image, or Bluetooth which offers wireless connection to a laptop or tablet. HDMI may also carry audio to the projector's audio system or to a PA. Bluetooth connection between laptop and projector is also increasingly available, but even if you plan to use Bluetooth, it would be advisable to have a cable connection handy, just in case. If you think you might need to buy a projector, make a careful choice — good ones are expensive.

## Digital Whiteboard

See Electronic Whiteboard

## Disc Jockey (DJ)

A person hosting a music program on radio, or presenting music for a social event such as a party, wedding, etc. The term was originally applied in the days when most music was on vinyl disc, and these were played in the studio.

## Discrete Variable

A discrete variable changes between one value and another in steps. Parcels and bricks are examples — they are counted, but not measured.

## Dropbox

A file-sharing system that allows invited participants access to the files placed in a folder. Google Drive offers a similar service.

## DVD

Originally the initials stood for Digital Video Disc, but Digital Versatile Disc is now more usually accepted. A DVD has a capacity of 4.7GB, and so can hold far more data than a CD. Like the CD, there are versions that can be read only, or can be recorded once, or be recorded and rewritten.

## Electronic Whiteboard

A computer with a large, high-resolution touchscreen display and dedicated software for collaborative working. Also known as a Digital Whiteboard, or Interactive Whiteboard.

## Engagement Techniques

Engagement techniques help you to build a relationship with your audience by involving them.

## Equalization

Equalization is a filtering process applied to audio. Settings such as "small speakers" can apply extra bass to compensate for the lack of bass. Other settings will be appropriate for the spoken word, and for different styles of music. Applying equalization is subjective. Bear in mind the need for clarity and intelligibility.

## Fee Structure

If you are a professional speaker, people need to know what it costs to hire you. What is your basic fee or fee structure? Does your fee vary according to the time of year or day? Does your fee include travel and subsistence costs? Under what circumstances do you speak pro bono? Do you expect to sell your own materials at a meeting or a conference? Etc.

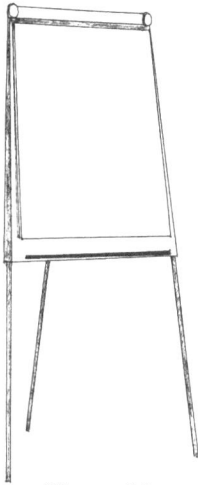

*Figure 89*

## Flip Chart

A pad of large paper sheets, typically around 64 cm x 75 cm (25 inches x 30 inches).

The pad is usually hung on a whiteboard or easel. The most popular format is blank paper, but lined and squared paper is also available. Some have an adhesive strip, Post-it style so they can be detached and stuck on a wall.

## Flip Chart Index

A technique of using small 'Post-its' as tabs to provide an index system for a set of flip chart pages. Each page has a 'Post-it' fixed to one side, and successive pages have them staggered so that all can be seen at once. This is especially useful if the presenter starts with the pages over the back of the easel and brings them forward in succession so that with the last page in place, all the tabs are visible. The technique then enables a presenter to select an individual page of the set with minimum fuss.

## Flow Chart

Diagram showing the movement of something. Road traffic flow is often shown with the road symbol thickened in proportion to the traffic volume. A production process chart can show the movement of components and of the final product. Flow charts may also show the movement of objects, ideas, cash, etc.

## FOH Lights

Front of house lights are used to light the audience area. FOH lights are usually dimmed at the start of a movie or stage play.

## FOH Sound

Front of house sound is the sound heard by the audience, usually controlled by a sound engineer positioned at the back of the room, or at the front of a balcony.

## Frequency Finder Site

A website that allows a wireless mike user to check which radio frequencies are in use in a local area. Users of wireless mikes are required to find and use frequencies that do not interfere with other radio users. http://sennheiser.us/freqfinder/index2.html

## Furry

A "furry" is a microphone windshield designed to minimize plosive sounds and wind rumble by preventing blasts of air from hitting the microphone's sensitive membrane. Also known as a wind muff.

## Gaffa Tape

Duct tape is a universal tool, but it may be worthwhile to consider gaffa (or gaffer) tape. It is widely used in the theatrical and TV industries because it holds well but can be removed easily, leaving no residue. Duct tape is cheaper, is better for long term application, but leaves a residue that may be a problem.

## Gestures

Gestures are dramatic poses and movements that reinforce a word or phrase and can help the presenter to convey a specific part of a message. One of the best-known gestures is the hand held out with the palm toward someone, universally understood as indicating 'stop'.

## Ghost image

A technique for chalkboards and flip charts in which an important image is drawn lightly on the chalkboard or flip chart prior to the presentation. Since the image is visible to the presenter, but not to the audience, the presenter can draw the image quickly and accurately following the 'ghost image' — thereby impressing the audience.

## GIF

The Graphics Interchange Format, more commonly referred to as a GIF, is an image format developed in 1987 for the Compuserve Bulletin Board. The format is now widely used on websites, text messages, video games, etc., and can be incorporated into presentations.

## Google Drive

A file-sharing system that allows invited participants access to the files placed in a folder. Dropbox offers a similar service.

## Google Slides

Presentation software from the Google Docs stable.

## Gooseneck

A short flexible metal stand attached to a conventional mike stand or to a baseplate fixed to a lectern. A mike holder is attached to the end of the gooseneck. The flexibility allows the mike position to be adjusted quickly and easily (though not always noiselessly) to accommodate different speakers.

## Gripping Stuff

A double-sided material that can be stuck on a wall and allows card and paper to stick to it. Also available in tape form. Useful for temporary displays since it can be removed easily without marking the wall.

## Handouts

Printed pages given to, or available to the audience at a presentation.

## Hardware

Items such as projectors, computers, cameras and phones are considered hardware. To make them operate, they rely on computer programs or software. The people who work with the hardware and software are sometimes referred to as liveware.

## HDMI

High-Definition Multimedia Interface, which most people know as the modern connection between a computer and a TV or projector. HDMI connections can carry both image and sound, and the connectors are small, making the format popular for home theater use.

*Figure 90*

## Hierarchies

An arrangement of ideas, steps or other data to show ascending layers. Most commonly seen in an organization where certain jobs or positions imply authority and responsibility for those below, but can also show ascending layers of a production process, of ideas, etc.

## Infographics

Many people find statistics confusing and overwhelming, and infographics aim to show data in a concise, easily understood way. Infographics can also be used to illustrate and complement a story.

## Interactive Whiteboard

See Electronic Whiteboard

## iTunes

iTunes was a media player, media library, and mobile device management application developed by Apple Inc. It was used to store, play, download, and organize digital audio, video, and ebooks on personal computers running the OS X and Microsoft Windows operating systems. Now super-seded by Music and other specialized software.

## Keynote

Presentation graphics software for Apple that allows a sequence of images, and the inclusion of audio and video. Keynote can read PowerPoint files.

## Keystoning

Distortion that happens when the projected image is not properly aligned with the screen. The most common form is a vertical distortion that makes the top of the image wider than the foot so that it resembles the shape of the keystone in an arch. If the projector is slightly to the side, key-stoning may be seen from left to right.

## Laser Pointer

A small low-powered laser device. The beam is usually invisible, and the small dot created by the beam makes it useful for pointing out detail on a screen or object. Red lasers are common, but a green laser may be more visible and thus more effective as a pointer.

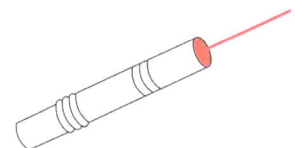

*Figure 91*

**Layering**

A technique of arranging overlapping images for effect, such as reveal and conceal.

**Lectern**

A lectern was originally a stand with a slanted platform on which a book could be placed and read. Lecterns come in tabletop and free-standing versions. Today a lectern could be a simple basic stand, or could include controls for audio, video, lighting, etc. The term is sometimes also applied to a podium, so if arranging to present (at a conference for example) it can be important to be sure of the distinction and hence of the precise facility available.

**Libre Office**

Open-source (free) presentation software.

**Lions**

Lions Clubs International. An international secular service club with members in over two hundred countries. Their meetings are an opportunity for presenters.

**Liveware**

Items such as projectors, computers, cameras and phones are considered hardware. To make them operate, they rely on computer programs or software. The people who work with the hardware and software are sometimes referred to as liveware.

**Mac**

A common term for any of the Apple family of computers.

**Microphone (Mike or Mic)**

A transducer that converts sound into very small electrical signals.

**MP3**

A format for audio files which greatly reduces their size while retaining most of the quality. This enables portable players such as smartphone to carry far more music than would otherwise be the case. As a rule of thumb, one minute of stereo sound takes about 1mB of file space.

**Multimedia**

Media and content in a variety of forms. For example, the spoken word may be augmented by the written (or projected) word, an image, a sound, or a video clip.

**Multiplatform**

Describes software that can be run on Windows or Mac computers.

**Nameplate**

A folded card, usually US letter or A4 size, on which your name is printed and displayed, typically at meetings. More permanent versions, made of wood, brass, acrylic, etc., are often used on desks.

## National Speakers Association (NSA)

An organization of professional speakers whose expertise covers a broad range of topics, skills, knowledge and experience. An important resource for the professional speaker.

## NeoOffice

Open-source (free) presentation software.

## Neutral stance

A slightly relaxed stance which conveys no significant message (unlike standing at attention or an athlete poised on a starting block).

## Organizational Chart

Diagrams that lay out the structure of an organization, or the flow of responsibilities, or of interaction.

## Overhead Projector

The Overhead Projector or OHP projects images from a flat light table over the shoulder of the presenter to a screen behind the presenter. The OHP enables the presenter to face the audience while working. OHP technology is cheap, versatile and reliable, and easy to use. Once in widespread use, the OHP has largely been displaced by whiteboards, laptop computers, and digital projectors.

## Overhead transparencies

Thin transparent sheets, sometimes called "slides," that are used on an Overhead Projector (OHP). The thinnest can be regarded as disposable, but thicker ones are more durable and can stand repeated use. Transparencies can be written on using marker pens designed for the purpose. Some are designed for printer use so that images or prepared text can be printed on them.

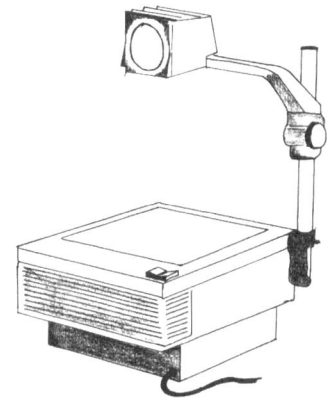

*Figure 92*

## PA

see Public Address

## Panache

Panache can be defined as flamboyance or flair, but in presentation terms, I prefer to think of it as a confident manner. The confidence comes with preparation and practice, thus mastering the practicalities.

## PC

A personal computer that uses the Microsoft system, such as Windows.

## Pizazz

An appealing combination of flair and glamour, helping to make your presentations stand out even more and be even more successful.

## Planner

A system for developing and delivering a presentation. The planner can be helpful in deciding content, running order, and timing, and a summary can be useful as a prompt during delivery.

## Plosives

The 'p' and 'b' sounds are the plosives. They produce puffs of air that can overload a microphone and produce unpleasant noises in a recording or PA system.

## Podium

A low platform on which a performer or speaker may stand to be more visible and be more clearly heard. The term is sometimes also applied to a lectern, so if arranging to present (at a conference for example) it can be important to be sure of the distinction and hence of the precise facility available.

## PowerPoint

Presentation graphics software for PCs that allows a sequence of images, and the inclusion of audio and video.

## Presentation

Communication with a purpose. A presentation can be to an audience of any size, from an individual upwards. It can be in a relatively informal setting such as meeting a colleague in a corridor, to the formality of the conference stage. The key to any presentation is its purpose, which is usually to inform, or persuade, and sometimes even just to entertain. The key to a successful presentation is clarity of purpose, and some presentation skills.

## Presentation Aids

Any device or technique that assists in achieving the purpose of the presentation.

## Presentation Pyramid

A graphic representation of the hierarchies of skills involved in a successful presentation.

## Presenter

A person who designs and delivers a presentation. The term is also applied in radio and television to the person hosting a radio or television program or show.

## Prezi

An online and fee-based alternative to Keynote or PowerPoint.

## Projection

In presentation terms, projection of the voice enables it to be heard at the back of the room. Projection is also the system of throwing an image onto a screen, usually from a digital projector.

## Prop

A theatrical property, or prop, is something used by actors on stage to help the audience understand the setting and/or plot. Yorick's skull in Shakespeare's *Hamlet* is a good example. Without it, Hamlet's speech would be less effective.

**Public Address, or PA**

A system of equipment whose purpose is to enable a person to be heard in a large space such as an auditorium. The three main components are:

1. a microphone, which converts sound into a tiny electrical signal, accurately
2. an amplifier which greatly increases the power of the electrical signal, accurately
3. a loudspeaker which converts the electrical signal from the amplifier back into sound, also accurately

The ideal PA makes the voice (or music) louder, without sacrificing audio quality.

**Public Speaking**

The process of speaking to a group of people in a structured and deliberate manner.
The purpose may be to inform, influence, or entertain the audience. Public speaking is intrinsic to presentation, although presentations can often be delivered to an audience of one.

**Radio Mike**

See Wireless Mike

**Rear Projection**

A technique of projecting onto a screen from behind so that the light diffuses the light through the screen. The image has to be reversed to be readable. Normal screens for front projection reflect the light.

**Rehearse**

To practice. How to rehearse is a matter for the individual. Some prefer to have a basic outline, think on their feet, and be spontaneous. Others prefer meticulous planning and rehearsal.

**Remote Control**

A remote control device enables a presenter to move from slide to slide in PowerPoint or Keynote without being tied to the laptop keyboard. A typical remote control has buttons to change forward and backwards. Some enable the screen to be blanked. Many incorporate a laser pointer. Most communicate to a small USB receiver, and setup is really simple — plug the receiver into the laptop, and switch on the remote control. Some smartphone applications also enable remote control, but have to be on the same wifi network as the laptop.

**Reveal Sheet**

A sheet of paper that can be used on an overhead projector to conceal part of an image, and removed to reveal the entire image. The technique can also be used on a flip chart page, using Post-its for small conceals, or a small sheet of paper taped in place. A similar effect can be achieved on a Keynote or PowerPoint presentation using layering.

## Reverberation

The time taken for sound to reach the back of a room and for the echo to return to you. In a large space with highly reflective surfaces, such as a gymnasium, the reverberation will be longer and quite noticeable. An equally large space with soft non-reflective surfaces, such as a theater, will have a shorter reverberation. Any empty space will have less reverberation when that same space is full of people.

## Reverse Projection

A technique which involves projecting an image on the rear of a translucent screen so that it is seen the right way round by the viewers at the front. The light path is to be "folded" using internal mirrors to save space. Reverse projection units were once used at exhibitions and conferences, but as flat-screen TV prices have fallen, they have largely disappeared.

## Rotarians

Members of Rotary International, an international secular service club with members in over two hundred countries. Rotary meetings are an opportunity for presenters. The standard time available is 20 to 30 minutes.

## Route Map

An initial image that sets out the stages of your presentation. More useful with smaller groups when it can be written on a flip chart and left in view. A presenter can use it to help an audience chart progress.

## Rule of Seven

A rule for projected text in a presentation that suggest a maximum of seven lines of text per image, and seven words per line. Make those seven lines and seven words big enough to be clearly visible to everyone in your audience.

## Shockmount

A microphone holder that is designed to absorb mechanical noise coming up through the mike stand. Especially useful if there is a risk of bumping into a floor stand, or a lectern mounted mike.

## Sightlines

Sightlines represent the unobstructed view each member of an audience has of the presenter, or the screen, or whatever is essential to the event. Sightlines may be obstructed by support pillars or columns in the room, or for individuals, by other people sitting in front of them.

## SlideShare

An online source of presentations. An area where you can exercise your critical skills, and a good source of ideas.

## Smartboard

A TV touch-screen development of the electronic whiteboard. See Electronic Whiteboard.

## Smartphone

Today, smartphones are everywhere. Many can carry presentation software for display on a projector to TV set. Many will also have applications that allow you to use the phone as a remote control for a presentation. Usually the laptop computer and the phone have to be on the same network, which is an extra complication you may wish to avoid. When the remote application works, it's wonderful, but the safer move may be to use a remote control with a USB receiver. Most of these are plug and play, and many include a laser pointer.

## Software

Items such as projectors, computers, cameras and phones are considered hardware. To make them operate, they rely on computer programs or software. The people who work with the hardware and software are sometimes referred to as liveware.

## Speaker Agreement

An arrangement that spells out the fee for a speaker and any other relevant conditions. For example, it might include or exclude travel and subsistence for the speaker, or specify that the speaker should not include marketing messages in the delivery of the presentation.

## Speakers Bureau

Usually an organization that provides speakers for others such as conference organizers. Sometimes an organization will have its own speakers bureau offering speakers relating to its own specific business or area of interest.

## Streaming Stick

A small device (several are comparable in size to a thumb drive) that plugs into the HDMI input on a TV and allows the screen of a smartphone or tablet to be shared.

## Technology

Technology includes tools and systems, processes and techniques. For our purposes it includes the humble pencil and the water-based marker, the techniques of planning and delivery, the overhead projector and the flip chart, the computer and the projector. It also includes the presenter's skills and qualities, creativity and sense of purpose.

## Teleprompter

A teleprompter is a screen on which is projected the text for a speech or news item. Placed in front of the camera lens, it enables the newsreader to see the teleprompter screen while maintaining eye contact with the lens, and hence the viewer. Any major politician giving a major speech will usually use two teleprompter screens, off to each side and slightly in front of the speaker. The two are synchronized, so the speaker can glance from one to the other, thus ensuring eye contact with the entire audience. All the audience sees is a small piece of glass, angled and at the speaker's eye level. The speaker sees an image projected onto the glass. It takes some practice to use, and is largely a tool of newsreaders and politicians.

**Toast**

Software that allows the creation of CDs and DVDs. Data files can be organized before transferring (or 'burning') to CD or DVD.

**Toastmasters**

Toastmasters International is a nonprofit educational organization that teaches public speaking and leadership skills through a worldwide network of clubs. Focused mainly on speeches, but useful to anyone who has to speak to an audience.

**Treasury Tag**

A treasury tag is a short piece of string with plastic or metal bars at either end. It is commonly used to hold papers or cards together by threading one end through punched holes. A single tag can hold a small bundle of suitably punched papers, and three tags can hold papers punched for a ring binder. Twist ties and rubber bands can be used instead, but are less robust. These are hard to find in the US.

*Figure 94*

**Underware**

Underware is a term I coined in 2004 to represent anything in a presentation that the audience shouldn't have to see. Go to the movies and you don't expect to see anything on the screen until the opening shot. (In the days before digital projectors, if the projectionist wasn't on the ball, sometimes one could see a countdown on the leader of the film.) Similarly, a PowerPoint presentation should start with the title frame. The audience shouldn't have to see the presenter's desktop and folders while the relevant file is sought. With OHP work, the audience shouldn't see the slides moving off and on the light table. Every presentation has a purpose, and so the presenter needs to avoid showing the audience anything which distracts them and inhibits that purpose, i.e., Don't Show Your Underware!

**US Letter**

A standard page size in the USA, roughly equivalent to the A4 size.
A US letter page is 11.0 inches long and 8.5 inches wide.
One A4 page is 29.7cm x 21.0cm, or 11.69 inches long and 8.27 inches wide.

**USB**

Universal Serial Bus. A standard connection on a computer that allows a range of external devices to be connected, and in some cases, powered. Hard drives, flash drives, CD drives, memory card adaptors, cameras and microphones can all be connected. There are now several types of USB connectors. USB C, the latest and fastest standard, allows very high data transfer speeds, but older and slower devices can still be used. USB C also carries audio and video (HDMI) data.

*Figure 95*

## Venue

The place where a presentation will be delivered. Venues range from conference halls to class-rooms, from theaters to offices, from corridors to boardrooms, from town halls to libraries, etc.

## VGA

Video Graphics Array. Most people knew it simply as the con-nector from a desktop computer to a display such as a screen or a projector. A VGA connection carries display information, but not sound, which is why it has largely been replaced by HDMI connections. VGA connectors are also bulky, taking up valuable space in today's small laptops. Modern MacBooks are thinner than a VGA connector.

*Figure 96*

## Video Conference

A video conference links participants via the internet so that they can both see and hear each other. 'Zoom' and 'Microsoft Teams' are examples in widespread use.

## Visual Aid

Anything that a presenter can show to the audience to help make a point or increase understanding.

## Voice Clipping

A situation in which the signal from a microphone overloads the input stage, producing audible distortion.

## WAV

A format for high quality audio files. As a rule of thumb, one minute of stereo sound needs about 10 MB of file space.

## Welcome Message

A simple message welcoming people to the event. This can be written on a flip chart and posi-tioned at the door, or placed to the side at the front, near the presenter.

## Whiteboard

A range of names apply, but the whiteboard is a rigid glossy board for non-permanent writing and marking. A whiteboard is cleaner and more color friendly than chalkboard, and can double as a projection screen.
Another form of whiteboard is the interactive digital whiteboard, but this is more often used by individuals or small workshop groups.

## Wind Muff

A cover for a microphone that protects it from plosive sounds and gusts of wind, both of which are likely to overload the sensitive membrane in the microphone, generating unpleasant sounds in the loudspeakers. Foam wind muffs are common, but the cheaper ones serve little purpose. See '"Furry."

## Windshield
Another name for a wind muff.

## WiFi
WiFi or Wi-Fi is a term used to describe a wireless local area network. The networked area might be a home, a library, a hotel or conference center, airport or train station, etc. The WiFi network is usually connected to the internet, but need not be.

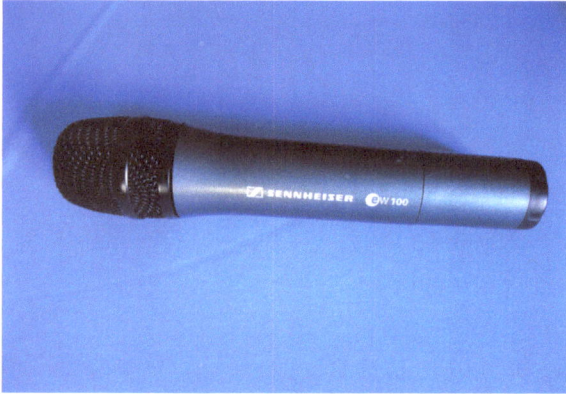

*Figure 97. Wireless Mike*

*Figure 98. Wireless transmitter/Receiver*

## Wireless Mike
A wireless microphone system converts audio from the mike into a radio signal which can be sent to a nearby receiver and fed into a PA or recording system. The transmitter may be built into the mike body, or separate, allowing a variety of mikes to be used. The separate transmitter can be clipped to a waist belt or placed in a shirt pocket.

## XLR
A robust locking connector used in professional standard equipment. The system is simple. A female XLR is always an input, and a male XLR is always an output.

## Zoom
Multiplatform (and ubiquitous) video conference software that allows presenters to work with a remote and dispersed audience.

*Figure 99*

# APPENDICES

# Appendix A. Basic Planner Page

| Intro | Part 1 | Part 2 | Part 3 | Part 4 | Conclusion | |
|-------|--------|--------|--------|--------|------------|---|
| | | | | | | |
| Elapsed Time | | | | | | |

*TABLE 13*

# Appendix B. How Good am I?

*One example. Note that the stages are entirely personal. You decide what they are for you There is no external standard involved.*

## HOW GOOD AM I AT – HANDLING QUESTIONS

| Stages | My definitions | What I need to do to move up one stage |
|---|---|---|
| Four – the best that I can realistically expect | I am comfortable with questions related to my purpose both during the presentation and after | |
| Three – acceptable, but I can do a little better | I can handle as many questions as time allows at the end and am choosy about questions during the presentation | To reach here I need to:<br>• rehearse my presentation well enough to be able to stop and resume<br>• write my planner clearly enough to be seen from farther away than usual<br>• work on self-confidence – I can do this! |
| Two – acceptable, but I can do much better | I can handle four or five questions at the end and prefer not to have any during the presentation | I am here |
| One – the minimum that I can accept | I limit questions to two or three at the end but not during the presentation | |

*TABLE 14*

Appendices

# Appendix C. Topics for "How Good Am I?"

## ADD ANY OTHERS THAT YOU CONSIDER USEFUL

| | |
|---|---|
| Adjusting language to the audience | Practicalities–creating handouts |
| Anxiety | Practicalities – mikes and PA systems |
| Aspiration (in relation to presentation skills) | Practicalities – room setup |
| Body language | Practicalities – staging and props |
| Competence (overall) | Practicalities – taking the stage |
| Confidence | Practicalities – use of flip chart |
| Content selection | Practicalities – use of OHP |
| Creating handouts | Practicalities – use of whiteboard |
| Creativity | Presenting via Zoom |
| Designing PowerPoint/Keynote sequences | Publicity |
| Defining a presentation purpose | Selecting aids |
| Evaluating my presentation | Speaking/delivery |
| Graphical skills | Technique selection |
| Handling questions | Timing – during delivery |
| Marketing | Timing – planning delivery |
| Planning – specific to presentation | Topic knowledge |
| Planning long term (calendar management, travel arrangements, etc.) | Topic related vocabulary |
| Practicalities – competence with relevant software | Versatility (able to present for many purposes/on many topics) |
| Practicalities – computer and projector | Vocal mannerisms |

*TABLE 15*

Appendices

# Appendix D. Underware – Some Examples

*You've probably seen many of these already, perhaps even been guilty of one or two. Normally none of them are fatal to a presentation, but all of them are distractions from your purpose, and so can make the difference between success and failure.*

- presenter not easily visible to audience

- presenter has to arrange/organize notes before starting

- projector image not in focus and has to be adjusted

- screen not lined up correctly so the image is keystoned

- audience sees blank projected image on screen before title slide

- audience sees computer desktop before the presentations starts (the classic, and the most common)

- audience shown a presentation in Navigator /Edit mode

- sound check not carried out prior to start

- presenter stands in the projected image, casting shadow on screen

- presenter stands in the projected image, obscuring it for some

- projector not switched on before start and takes time to warm up

- projector left on too long, showing redundant image

- notes on noisy paper causing distraction when moved

- mike needs to be adjusted/moved to right place

- presenter notes in wrong place

- visual aid or prop visible before it becomes relevant

- presenter has to make major adjustments to audio system before beginning

# Appendix E. Other Reading

There are many books on presentation skills. Here are just a few, in alphabetical order, with no implied recommendation or endorsement.

- ✓ *Effective Presentation Skills, Revised Edition: A Practical Guide for Better Speaking*, by Steve Mandel

- ✓ *GRAB 'EM! The Guide to Killer Presentation Skills (The fundamentals of communication Book 1)*, by Reinoud Van Rooij

- ✓ *How to Create Amazing Presentations: The Public Speakers Guide to being engaging, Inspiring, and Unforgettable*, by David Bishop

- ✓ *How to Make Presentations That Teach and Transform*, by Robert J. Garmston and Bruce M. Wellman

- ✓ *How to Prepare, Stage and Deliver Winning Presentations*, by Thomas Leech

- ✓ *How to Write and Give a Speech*, by Joan Detz

- ✓ *Magic of Public Speaking: A Complete System to Become a World Class Speaker*, by Andrii Sedniev

- ✓ *Presentations: Secrets to World Class Presentations, That Move, Inspire, and Transform*, by John Higher

- ✓ *Presentation Skills 201: How to take it to the next level as a Confident, Engaging Presenter*, by William E. Steele

- ✓ *Presentation Skills: How to give great talks without fear (Instant Guides)*, by Chris Croft

- ✓ *Presentation Skills: How to Make a Great Presentation*, by Liam Lusk

- ✓ *Speaking from the Top*, by Tony Leary

- ✓ *The Articulate Executive*, by Granville Toogood

- ✓ *Why Most PowerPoint Presentations Suck…. And how you can make them better*, by Rick Altman

# Appendix F. Printable Checklists

## I. AGREEMENT CHECKLIST

### CONTACT DETAILS

| Name | | Company | |
|------|---|---------|---|
| Position | | Address 1 | |
| Tel | | Address 2 | |
| Email | | Post/Zip code | |
| Other | | | |

Fee

Extras

**WHEN:** Date(s)                    Time(s)

**WHO:** Audience composition and number

**WHAT:** Purpose of presentation, objectives

1.

2.

3.

**WHERE**: Venue

Name

Address

Phone Number

Parking

Size: Auditorium? Conference room?

Facilities: Stage, podium, lectern, lighting, audio, etc.

**HOW:** Suggested style or format

Logistics: What needs to be there, what do I need to bring

Travel details

Resources

## 2. SAFETY CHECKLIST

### Equipment Containers *(bags, boxes, crates)*

- ❏ Equipment Containers (bags, boxes, crates)
- ❏ Containers safe and secure
- ❏ Containers clearly labeled for shipping, storing, etc.
- ❏ No containers too heavy to lift or carry
- ❏ No sharp corners or edges
- ❏ Carry handles secure and comfortable
- ❏ Castors working, free to swivel, wheels free to rotate
- ❏ Clasps, catches and locks working properly (where fitted)

### Equipment

- ❏ Fuses at correct rating (and spares)
- ❏ Lenses dust free and focusing properly
- ❏ Casings free of sharp edges or other projections
- ❏ Power switches operating properly
- ❏ Cooling fans operating properly
- ❏ Fan ducts free of dust and fluff
- ❏ All batteries fresh, and spares available

### Power Cords

- ❏ Cords in good condition with no frayed, worn or chafed sections.
- ❏ Connectors in good condition with no breaks or cracks
- ❏ Outlet strips/extensions fitted with switches and neon indicators

### Connecting Cords for audio, laptop etc.

- ❑ Cords in good condition with no frayed, worn or chafed sections
- ❑ Securely plugged in
- ❑ Safely tied or routed
- ❑ In power cord covers wherever possible
- ❑ Taped down with gaffa tape if necessary

### Room

- ❑ Emergency exits clearly visible
- ❑ Emergency exits unobstructed
- ❑ Fire extinguishers available
- ❑ Fire alarm procedure available and known
- ❑ Nearest fire alarm location known
- ❑ Breaker box location known
- ❑ Lighting switch locations known
- ❑ Emergency lighting operational
- ❑ All furniture in safe condition (tables, chairs)
- ❑ Carpeting or floor covering safe with no worn or loose areas
- ❑ Seating capacity known and not reached
- ❑ Seating layout allows safe access and egress
- ❑ Coffee and other catering safely available

### Dress

- ❑ Identity badge, necklace etc., on quick release safety clasp
- ❑ No loose or flowing clothing to catch on furniture or equipment
- ❑ Footgear secure – no loose laces or stiletto heels

## 3. PRESENTER'S PLANNING CHECKLIST

**Speaker Agreement**
- ❑ Who is the client?
- ❑ What is the topic or purpose?
- ❑ When is the presentation – date and time?
- ❑ Who is the audience?
- ❑ Where is the venue?
- ❑ How to get there?
- ❑ What is the fee?
- ❑ How are expenses to be met?
- ❑ How will payment be made?
- ❑ When will payment be paid?
- ❑ What evaluation will be carried out?

**Before the Event**
- ❑ Good advance notice _ you need: full details of purpose and title
  - ❑ size and character of audience
  - ❑ precise venue location and details
  - ❑ facilities available, etc.
- ❑ Check two or three days before event to confirm arrangements
- ❑ Provide material for your own introduction to audience

**Materials**
- ❑ Don't rely on voice alone
- ❑ Use appropriate pictures (flip chart, PowerPoint, etc. gestures, good, appropriate jokes
- ❑ Engagement devices; e.g., small gifts and awards
- ❑ Handouts, etc.

**OHP Slides**
- ❑ All mounted, preferably in 3M professional holders
- ❑ All with same orientation, preferably landscape
- ❑ Clear and simple layout, not overcrowded

**PowerPoint Presentation**
- ❑ All with same orientation, preferably landscape
- ❑ Clear and simple layout, not overcrowded
- ❑ Simple, consistent animations, and no sound effects
- ❑ Audio and video checked
- ❑ Remote control checked

## Flip Charts
- ❏ Do some need to be pre-drawn?
- ❏ Preparation time on the day to draw up

## Audio
- ❏ Check sound, but know not to blow into mike
- ❏ Stay within mike pickup area
- ❏ Audio clips clearly identified, cued, scripted, etc.

## Video
- ❏ Check projector/TV connection
- ❏ Video clips clearly identified, cued, scripted, etc.

## Structure
- ❏ Use "route map" to introduce
- ❏ Let audience read slides
- ❏ Handouts with space for notes
- ❏ Listen to audience and wait for them
- ❏ Punctuate, perhaps by referring to "route map"
- ❏ Offer summary to finish
- ❏ Clean clear ending

## Organization
- ❏ Arrive early to check facilities
- ❏ Resolve not to show underware
- ❏ Check focus, image size, of any projector to be used
- ❏ Arrive early to meet audience members, organizers, etc.
- ❏ Good positioning – clearly visible to audience
- ❏ Cover flip chart pages after use
- ❏ "Neutral" stance whenever possible
- ❏ Move only when necessary
- ❏ Make good eye contact with audience
- ❏ Use planner or notes – don't read lengthy text
- ❏ Have notes or script available for any helper needed
- ❏ Script adjusted for purpose and audience – not just repeat of a previous presentation
- ❏ Use clear positive gestures, well held

## 4. PRESENTER'S KIT

### Flip Chart
- ❏ Flip chart pad with spare pages for writing
- ❏ Spare pad just in case
- ❏ Easel(s)
- ❏ Marker pens, chisel point, black, red, green, blue
- ❏ Small "Post-its" to use as tabs for pages
- ❏ Magic tape for emergency repairs
- ❏ Pointer – 60 centimeters to 1 meter (two to three feet) long
- ❏ Laser pointer and spare batteries

### Whiteboard
- ❏ Marker pens, chisel point, black, red, green, blue
- ❏ Eraser pad
- ❏ Pointer or ruler, 60 centimeters to 1 meter (2 to 3 feet) long

### Data Projector
- ❏ Laptop
- ❏ Laptop charger and cable
- ❏ Phone charger and cable
- ❏ Backup CD or USB drive of presentation material
- ❏ Connecting cables – audio, VGA, HDMI
- ❏ Bongo ties or other cable fasteners
- ❏ Remote control – USB based, Bluetooth, or smartphone
- ❏ Power cables – always have an extension available (at least five meters or 15 feet)
- ❏ Laser pointer and spare batteries
- ❏ HDMI to VGA convertor if necessary

### Audio
- ❏ Your own microphone
- ❏ Cables, XLR extension cable(s)
- ❏ Audio output cable for laptop, typically 3.5mm jack to RCA phono or XLR

### Miscellaneous
- ❏ Fresh batteries for anything that needs them
- ❏ Little clock, or phone app, to place on table or lectern
- ❏ Scissors
- ❏ Lump of BluTak and/or roll of "Gripping Stuff"

- ❏ Laser pointer
- ❏ Roll of gaffa tape
- ❏ Blu Tack blob to hold pointer
- ❏ Spare fuse for any equipment that needs one
- ❏ 2″ or 3″ ring binder – the bigger one holds more. This is a handy way of storing notes,
- ❏ OHP slides, your presentation layout, etc.

**Notes**
- ❏ Index cards
- ❏ Post-it pad
- ❏ Planner page
- ❏ Nameplate (always bring your own – at least your name will be spelled correctly)
- ❏ **Business cards** – always have plenty.
- ❏ **Fee structure** – (if appropriate) – never travel without it.
- ❏ **Diary or calendar** – showing available dates (just in case).
- ❏ **Speaker checklist** – for this event.

## 5. VENUE CHECKLIST

**BEFORE THE EVENT**
Inquiry/booking stage
Send speaker pack with
- ❑ Description of event
- ❑ Location of venue
- ❑ Directions on reaching location
- ❑ Room size and orientation – does it get direct sunlight?
- ❑ Suggested seating plan
- ❑ List of facilities – screen, projector, PA, etc.

**1 week before event**
- ❑ Call to check all is well/clarify needs/fill gaps. etc.
- ❑ Ask for material to use in introduction

**FACILITIES**
List of what is available as part of speaker package; i.e., we provide screen and lectern with fixed mike.

**OHP/Projection Screen**
- ❑ Position screen leaning out at top to eliminate keystoning
- ❑ Have standard position for OHP or other projector to ensure screen is well filled by image
- ❑ OHP pens available
- ❑ Weighted page available for reveals
- ❑ Pointer or arrow
- ❑ Use brakes to make sure trolley-mounted projector stays in place
- ❑ Projector controls clearly marked -– on/off, focus, lamp change
- ❑ Check focus

**Flip Charts**
- ❑ Set up on either side of screen
- ❑ Ensure plenty of sheets are left on the pad
- ❑ Have pens available on the easel ledge
- ❑ Standard cover page – "welcome to hotel/company/venue"

**PowerPoint and Projector**
- ❑ Invite speaker to send sample file in advance to check on venue computer
- ❑ Offer HDMI input from either end of meeting room
- ❑ Ensure projector properly adjusted – focus, image size, etc.

- ❏ Have remote control available to presenter or with assistant as required
- ❏ Check focus if projector is ceiling mounted

### Audio
- ❏ Check for mike preference – none, tieclip, stand mounted
- ❏ Check if recordings are to be included in presentation
- ❏ Check laptop / tablet connection to venue PA

### Lighting
- ❏ Specify lighting control availability
- ❏ Indicate window shades or curtains

### ORGANIZATION
- ❏ Arrive early to help speaker check facilities
- ❏ Provide good positioning – speaker clearly visible
- ❏ Provide pad of Post-its
- ❏ Have introduction notes – use planner
- ❏ Advise on pronunciation of names, titles, qualifications
- ❏ Have welcome message visible – screen, projector or flip chart
- ❏ Have side table for handouts or other items
- ❏ Provide clearly visible clock
- ❏ Be ready to link, thank, move people to coffee, etc., as appropriate

### AFTER THE EVENT
- ❏ Thank you letter to speaker
- ❏ Speaker feedback
- ❏ Agreed evaluation process – share results with speaker

# Index

# About the Author

Tom Laurenson started speaking in public at the age of 7, wining prizes for poetry recitation at county arts festivals. He was an educator in Scotland for over 30 years, working in the classroom, in technological innovation, and professional development. Moving to the USA, he worked with the Kitchawan Institute, developing workshops, presentations and a conference on solar energy. Tom finished his career working on professional development with Fordham University in the Bronx, New York, helping to encourage teachers to use computers in their classrooms. Tom is a long-standing Rotarian, and after moving to Branford, started the Branford Microfund, and runs a Speakers Bureau for the Shore Line Trolley Museum in Branford, Connecticut.

During his career he has designed and delivered presentations to audiences large and small, in venues large and small, on a wide range of topics and themes, and for a variety of purposes. As an experienced deliverer and careful observer of presentations, he became aware that many presentations didn't work as well as they might, mainly because of simple errors or omissions.

In writing this book, Tom has drawn on all of that experience, and provided a wealth of practical advice for anyone who ever has to design and deliver a presentation for any purpose. He believes that people have to build on their own particular attributes, and has worked to design a book from which each person can pick and choose what they need to improve their own presentations.

Tom is available to deliver presentations, workshops and coaching sessions via his website — www.tomlaurenson.com — or can be contacted by email, tom@tomlaurenson.com.

www.ingramcontent.com/pod-product-compliance
Lightning Source LLC
Chambersburg PA
CBHW050906210326
41597CB00002B/46